DEATH-BED VISIONS

DEATH-BED VISIONS

The Otherworldly Experiences of the Dying

Sir William Barrett

GREEN POINT BOOKS

For information, address:
Greenpoint Books, Ltd.
767 South 4th Street
Philadelphia, PA 19147
info@greenpointbooks.com

Paper: 979-8-88677-030-8
Cloth: 979-8-88677-031-5

Cover design
by Michael Schrauzer

CONTENTS

EDITOR'S PREFACE

THIS book is sent out to the public in an unfinished state. It will be seen that in the introduction the author has only sketched the line of discussion which he would have elaborated, and even this outline is incomplete.

The editor prefers, however, to leave untouched both the introduction and the discussion of cases, believing that by so doing the thought of the author will be more truly conveyed than would be the case were any elaboration undertaken by another hand. The outline was clearly unfinished, for several passages in the books of reference had been marked by him for discussion, and particularly paragraphs in Professor Bozzano's recently published book, " Phénomènes Psychiques au Moment de la Mort," translated from Italian to French by C. de Vesme (Editions de la B.P.S., 8 Rue Copernic [16c], Paris), 1923.

He was specially interested in Bozzano's observation that if the phenomena were caused by the thoughts of the dying person being directed to those he loved, the appearances might be expected to represent living persons at least as frequently as deceased persons who had long passed from this world, whereas no records had come to hand of dying persons seeing at their bedside visions of friends still living.

He would have liked to ask those who believe the visions to be the product of intense desire or thought to collect evidence in support of their theory, showing that desire for living friends may produce visions of them at the bedside seen *during moments of full consciousness*.

There are, no doubt, cases of so-called travelling clairvoyance (see Chapter IV), in which the dying persons, *after a period of trance or unconsciousness*, said they had seen living relatives at a distance ; and there was in some instances reciprocal vision by the distant relative of the figure of the dying person— usually mistaken for a real appearance. This is clearly a very different type of phenomenon.

Another point which the author had discussed with friends was that in the cases of phantasms of the living collected by the

Society for Psychical Research it has usually been the person thinking, and not the one thought of, whose image was projected in vision.

On this analogy, when a dying person sees the phantasm of one already deceased the initiative would appear to come from the thought of the latter, whose survival is thereby demonstrated.

He was greatly impressed by a feature not uncommon at the death-beds of young children, viz., the description of the vision in terms not in keeping with ideas arising from their religious upbringing. He considered that in such circumstances the hallucination could hardly be ascribed to a mere flight of fancy.

In arranging the groups of cases he gave the first place to those relating to visions of a deceased person whom the dying percipient did not know to be dead. A recent and striking experience was that of Mrs. B., the first narrative in Chapter II. He recognized that where the death was known to anybody present in the room an attempt might be made to stretch telepathy to cover the incident, but he maintained that such an explanation would not account for the cases in this chapter, in which the percipient and the bystanders were equally unaware of the death.

The author had given considerable time and thought to the subject, and looked forward to making the groups of cases as complete and representative as possible before publication. This, however, was not to be, for he himself, in the midst of active work, passed suddenly into " that little-known country " towards which his thought had so often taken wing.

He was anxious to prove that even people who have been sceptical all their lives of any survival after death have sometimes given evidence that at the very end they knew there was an after life.

He did not therefore choose material representing visions seen only by believers in survival of the soul, or by those with special psychic powers, but also visions seen by people with no belief in a future life (see cases at the end of Chapter III).

He put each case fairly, without keeping weak points in the background, and he left it to the reader himself to consider how far telepathy or some other mental attribute could be stretched to cover the circumstances. He expected impartial critics to realize that sometimes such an explanation would appear itself to involve a flight or extension of the soul incompatible with the material bounds of life.

It is hoped that this little book, though it falls short of what the author contemplated, will to some extent carry out his plan and direct attention in this country to phenomena which seemed to him to deserve more study than they have received.

The editor gratefully acknowledges the help given by Mr. Trethewy, in his careful reading of the manuscript, in preparation of the index and in many valuable suggestions.

F. E. B.

April 1926

DEATH-BED VISIONS

CHAPTER I

INTRODUCTION

IT is well known that there are many remarkable instances where a dying person,
shortly before his or her transition from the
earth, appears to see and recognize some
deceased relatives or friends. We must, however, remember the fact that hallucinations of
the dying are not very infrequent. Nevertheless, there are instances where the dying person
was *unaware* of the previous death of the spirit
form he sees, and is therefore astonished to
find in the vision of his or her deceased relative
one whom the percipient believes to be still
on earth. These cases form, perhaps, one of
the most cogent arguments for survival after
death, as the evidential value and veridical (truth telling) character of these Visions
of the Dying is greatly enhanced when
the fact is undeniably established that the
dying person was wholly ignorant of the
decease of the person he or she so vividly
sees.

With reference to these visions that eminent

physiologist of European fame, Prof. Richet, writes as follows :

" Facts of this kind are very important. They are much more explicable on the spiritist theory than by the hypothesis of mere cryptesthesia. Among all the facts adduced to prove survival, these seem to me to be the most disquieting (i.e. from a materialistic point of view). I have therefore thought it a duty to be scrupulous in mentioning them."

As is well known Prof. Richet does not believe in the existence of a soul, or of survival after death, and explains the evidence afforded by psychical research of a spiritual world by his theory of *cryptesthesia*, by which he means the perception of things or beings, by some sensory organ at present unknown to science, a faculty not possessed by every one, but, in my opinion, conclusively established to exist in certain individuals. These sensitives are to be found in all countries, in both sexes, and may be old or young, rich or poor, educated or ignorant. This faculty of clairvoyance—this vision of persons or things invisible to normal eyesight—may occur when the sensitive is quite conscious, but is more often observed in the trance condition, especially when this is induced by deep hypnosis—the " mesmeric trance " as it used to be called.

The older mesmerists employed the word "lucidity," or "travelling clairvoyance," for the perception of things at a distance. The term clairvoyance is, however, ambiguous, for it is now used in two different senses, namely, either for :

(a) The perception of hidden *material* objects remote from the sensitive, such as underground water ; or

(b) For the perception by the sensitive of *immaterial* objects, such as apparitions of deceased persons.

To avoid this confusion Myers suggested the term "telesthesia" instead of clairvoyance for the perception of material things. Telesthesia he defines as the sensation or perception of objects or conditions independently of the recognized channels of sense, and also independently of any possible telepathic communition as the source of the knowledge thus gained. Hence the term telesthesia would be inapplicable to apparitions of the dead or visions of the dying; whereas Richet would include both of these, as well as the vision of hidden material things, under his word "cryptesthesia," which appears to have the same connotation as the familiar word clairvoyance, and therefore it labours under the same ambiguity as that word.

Other terms for clairvoyance have been suggested ; in America Mr. Henry Holt uses the word " telopsis," and Dr. Heysinger the word " telecognosis " ; but these terms could hardly be applied to apparitions or visions of the dying, which appear near to, and not far from, the sensitive.

Miss Cobbe in her " Peak in Darien " makes some interesting remarks on the subject of Visions of the Dying. She states :

" The dying person is lying quietly, when suddenly, in the very act of expiring, he looks up— sometimes starts up in bed—and gazes on (what appears to be) vacancy, with an expression of astonishment, sometimes developing instantly into joy, and sometimes cut short in the first emotion of solemn wonder and awe. If the dying man were to see some utterly-unexpected but instantly-recognized vision, causing him a great surprise, or rapturous joy, his face could not better reveal the fact. The very instant this phenomenon occurs, Death is actually taking place, and the eyes glaze even while they gaze at the unknown sight."

As regards the general subject of Visions of the Dying, Mr. Myers has some interesting remarks in " Phantasms of the Living." He states that in his view such an occurrence " must probably often take place though it can seldom leave any record behind it. For here we have an account of that side only of a reciprocal incident which is usually lost to human knowledge altogether : I mean of the supernormal percipience of a man in the very article of death ; while there is no record of any corresponding sound or vision as experienced by those to whom he seemed to pay his visit of farewell.[1]

There are, however, several cases on record where the vision of those who have passed over is shared by friends at the bedside of the dying person. Instances of these will be given in a later chapter.

In considering the value of evidence for supernormal phenomena the importance of the cumulative character of the evidence must be taken into account. It is the undesigned coincidence of witnesses who have had no communication with each other that constitutes its value taken as a whole, whilst a single case may be doubtful or disproved, just as a single stick may be broken but a faggot may defy all our attempts at breaking a bundle of sticks.

On this point Archbishop Whately has some admirable remarks on the value of testimony. He states :

" It is evident that when many coincide in their testimony (where no previous concert can have

[1] " Phantasms of the Living," Vol. II, p. 305.

taken place), the probability resulting from this concurrence does not rest on the supposed veracity of each considered separately, but on the improbability of such an agreement taking place by chance. For though in such a case each of the witnesses should be considered as unworthy of credit, and even much more likely to speak falsehood than truth, still the chances would be infinite against their all agreeing in the same falsehood." [1]

About fifty years ago the learned incumbent of a church in Birmingham, the Rev. J. S. Pollock, published a collection of cases of supernormal phenomena under the curious title of " Dead and Gone."   Although some five hundred cases are quoted, taken from various sources, no attempt has been made at the investigation of any single case, so that the book as a whole has little evidential value.

Here I may quote some suggestive remarks made by Mrs. Henry Sidgwick soon after the foundation of the Society for Psychical Research, and published in the " Proceedings " for 1885 (p. 69) :

" Most of those to whom this paper is addressed probably belong to some Christian denomination, and to them the continued existence of the soul after death is, of course, no new theory invented to account for such phenomena as we are discussing,

---

[1] See Whately's " Rhetoric," Chapter I.

or requiring such phenomena to support it. But few will have any difficulty in agreeing with me that (1) the possibility of receiving [visions of or] communications from the dead, here and now, would not follow as a necessary consequence from the immortality of the soul; (2) that if communication of what I may call an objective kind— distinguishable, I mean, from our own thoughts and emotions—is possible to all those of the departed who desire it, we should naturally expect it to occur *more frequently* than the most sanguine can suppose that it actually does; and (3) that its possibility, while not in contradiction with any of the known facts of physical science, is certainly not supported, or in any way suggested, by any of these facts. However firmly, therefore, we may believe in the continued existence of dead human beings, we cannot regard the supposition of their action on the minds of the living as if it were merely the reference of an effect to a *vera causa* known to be adequate to produce it. We must treat it as we should treat the hypothesis—in any department of physical investigation—of an entirely new agent, for the existence of which we have no evidence outside the phenomenon which it is introduced to explain. If this be so, it will, I think, be admitted that we should be violating an established rule of scientific method if we introduced such a hypothesis except in the last resort, when all other modes of explanation seem clearly to fail.

" Exactly at what point of improbability this

failure of other explanations is to be regarded as established, cannot, I think, be defined—at any rate, I feel quite unable to define it. But I may perhaps say that, in my opinion, it is a point which can hardly be reached in the case of any narrative of a *single event* considered by itself : if we had only a *single* ghost-story to deal with, I can hardly conceive the kind or amount of evidence which would lead me to prefer the hypothesis of ghostly agency to all other possible explanations. The existence, therefore, of phantasms of the dead can only be established, if at all, by the accumulation of improbabilities in which we become involved by rejecting a large mass of apparently strong testimony to facts which, as recounted, would seem to admit of no other satisfactory explanation ; and in testing the value of this testimony we are bound, I think, to strain to the utmost all possible suppositions of recognized causes, before we can regard the narrative in question as even tending to prove the operation of this novel agency."

On the other hand, every scientific society ought to have as its motto the opinion expressed by Sir John Herschel in his discourse on " Natural Philosophy " (p. 127), " that the perfect observer . . . will have his eyes as it were opened that they may be struck at once with any occurrence which, according to received theories, ought *not* to happen ; for these are the facts which serve as clues to

new discoveries." Unfortunately, as Goethe
remarked in one of his conversations with
Eckermann, "in the sciences . . . if anyone
advances anything new . . . people resist with
all their might ; they speak of the new view
with contempt, as if it were not worth the
trouble of even so much as an investigation or
a regard ; and thus a new truth may wait a
long time before it can win its way."

CHAPTER II

VISIONS SEEN BY THE DYING OF PERSONS BY THEM UNKNOWN TO BE DEAD

THE evidence of Visions of the Dying, when they appear to see and recognize some of their relatives of whose decease they were unaware, affords perhaps one of the strongest arguments in favour of survival. Even Prof. Richet regards this evidence as impossible to explain by cryptesthesia. I have given some striking instances of these visions of the dying in my book " On the Threshold of the Unseen," and other cases will be found in the " Proceedings " of our Society.

A recent case of the kind was related to me by Lady Barrett, which occurred when she was in attendance on a patient in the Mothers' Hospital, at Clapton, of which she is one of the Obstretic Surgeons.

Lady Barrett received an urgent message from the Resident Medical Officer, Dr. Phillips, to come to a patient, Mrs. B., who was in labour and suffering from serious heart failure. Lady Barrett went at once, and the child was delivered safely, though the mother was dying at the time. After seeing other patients Lady Barrett went back to Mrs. B.'s ward, and the

10

following conversation occurred which was written down soon afterwards. Lady Barrett says :

" When I entered the ward Mrs. B. held out her hands to me and said, ' Thank you, thank you for what you have done for me—for bringing the baby. Is it a boy or girl ? ' Then holding my hand tightly, she said, ' Don't leave me, don't go away, will you ? ' And after a few minutes, while the House Surgeon carried out some restorative measures, she lay looking up towards the open part of the room, which was brightly lighted, and said, ' Oh, don't let it get dark—it's getting so dark . . . darker and darker.' Her husband and mother were sent for.

" Suddenly she looked eagerly towards one part of the room, a radiant smile illuminating her whole countenance. ' Oh, lovely, lovely,' she said. I asked, ' What is lovely ? ' ' What I *see*,' she replied in low, intense tones. ' What do you see ? ' ' Lovely brightness—wonderful beings.' It is difficult to describe the sense of reality conveyed by her intense absorption in the vision.

" Then—seeming to focus her attention more intently on one place for a moment—she exclaimed, almost with a kind of joyous cry, ' Why, it's Father ! Oh, he's so glad I'm coming ; he *is* so glad. It would be perfect if only W. (her husband) could come too.'

" Her baby was brought for her to see. She looked at it with interest, and then said, ' Do you think I ought to stay for baby's sake ? ' Then turning towards the vision again, she said, ' I can't —I can't stay ; if you could see what I do, you would know I can't stay.'

" But she turned to her husband, who had come in, and said, ' You won't let baby go to anyone who won't love him, will you ? ' Then she gently pushed him to one side, saying, ' Let me see the lovely brightness.'

" I left shortly after, and the Matron took my place by the bedside. She lived for another hour, and appeared to have retained to the last the double consciousness of the bright forms she saw, and also of those tending her at the bedside, e.g. she arranged with the Matron that her premature baby should remain in hospital till it was strong enough to be cared for in an ordinary household.

" (Signed)   FLORENCE E. BARRETT "

Dr. Phillips, who was present, after reading the above notes writes to me saying that she " fully agrees with Lady Barrett's account."

The most important evidence is however given by the Matron of the Hospital, who has sent the following account :

" I was present shortly before the death of Mrs. B., together with her husband and her mother. Her husband was leaning over her and speaking to her, when pushing him aside [1] she said, ' Oh, don't

---

[1] This is not the incident mentioned by Lady Barrett, but a later incident of the same kind.

hide it ; it's so beautiful.' Then turning away
from him towards me, I being on the other side of
the bed, Mrs. B. said, ' Oh, why there's Vida,'
referring to a sister of whose death three weeks
previously she had not been told. Afterwards the
mother, who was present at the time, told me, as
I have said, that Vida was the name of a dead sister
of Mrs. B.'s, of whose illness and death she was
quite ignorant, as they had carefully kept this news
from Mrs. B. owing to her serious illness.

" (Signed) MIRIAM CASTLE
" Matron "

I asked Dr. Phillips to try and obtain the
independent report of Mrs. B.'s mother, who,
as the Matron stated, was also present at the
time. This was kindly done, and I have received the following interesting and informative
letter from Mrs. Clark (Mrs. B.'s mother) :

HIGHBURY, N. 5.
" I have heard you are interested in the beautiful
passing of my dear daughter's spirit from this earth
on the 12th day of January, 1924.

" The wonderful part of it is the history of the
death of my dear daughter, Vida, who had been an
invalid some years. Her death took place on the
25th day of Dec., 1923, just 2 weeks and 4 days
before her younger sister, Doris, died. My
daughter Doris, Mrs. B., was very ill at that time,
and the Matron at the Mothers' Hospital deemed
it unwise for Mrs. B. to know of her sister's death.

Therefore when visiting her we put off our mourning and visited her as usual. All her letters were also kept by request until her husband had seen who they might be from before letting her see them. This precaution was taken lest outside friends might possibly allude to the recent bereavement in writing to her, unaware of the very dangerous state of her health.

" When my dear child was sinking rapidly, at first she said, ' It is all so dark ; I cannot see.' A few seconds after a beautiful radiance lit up her countenance ; I know now it was the light of Heaven, and it was most beautiful to behold. My dear child said, ' Oh, it is lovely and bright ; you cannot see as I can.' She fixed her eyes on one particular spot in the ward, saying, ' Oh, God, forgive me for anything I have done wrong.' After that she said, ' I can see Father ; he wants me, he is so lonely.' She spoke to her father, saying, ' I am coming,' turning at the same time to look at me, saying, ' Oh, he is so near.' On looking at the same place again, she said with rather a puzzled expression, ' He has Vida with him,' turning again to me saying ' Vida is with him.' Then she said, ' You do want me, Dad ; I am coming.' Then a very few parting words or sighs were expressed— nothing very definite or clear. With great difficulty and a very hard strain she asked to see ' the man who married us ' : this was to her husband, who was standing on the opposite side of the bed. His name she could not say ; it was the Rev. Maurice Davis, of All Saints, Haggerston, E., and he was sent for.[1] He had known my dear child for some years, and was so impressed by the vision that he quoted it in his ' Parish Magazine ' for February last.

" Yours respectfully

" (Signed) MARY C. CLARK "

Before passing on to other cases it is desirable to discuss somewhat in detail the foregoing case. The vision seen by the dying woman, Mrs. B., was obviously not due to her normal sight, otherwise the figures would have been seen by others present in the room ; the appearance therefore was not due to any ordinary material objects, nor is it likely to have been due to some illusion, that is to say, the misinterpretation of some object actually present to sight—as when a dressing-gown is mistaken for a woman—for not only was there nothing in the room to suggest such an illusion, but she recognized both her deceased father and sister, moreover she was quite unaware of the death of the latter. A more probable explanation is that it was an hallucination, which may be defined as " a sensory perception which has no objective counterpart within the field of vision." The question therefore becomes whether it was merely a delusive

[1] He came, but Mrs. B. had then become incapable of speech though still alive.

hallucination, when there *is* nothing whatever to which it corresponds, or a veridical hallucination—corresponding to some real event, which was invisible to normal eyesight. This must not be confused with a delusion, which applies to cases where there is *no* corresponding reality. There are many well-known cases of vivid illusions of sight which sometimes accompany the oncoming of sleep, as when a dream figure persists for a short time, or when faces in the dark are vividly seen by certain persons ; these illusions are termed hypnagogic. Externalized impressions of this kind are the frequent source of imaginary apparitions, such as occur to nervous people walking through lonely places at night time. To many of my readers this commonsense explanation will appear to be the origin of the vision of the dying which we have just related, the whole matter being dismissed as a mere coincidence. If this case stood alone this would be the probable explanation ; it will however be seen that mere chance coincidence cannot apply to the numerous cases which will be recited later on. Another explanation is the creation of hallucination in the percipient by some transference of thought or telepathic influence from those around the bedside. In the case just recited however this explanation fails for Lady Barrett and Dr.

Phillips knew nothing about the decease of the
percipient's father, when the latter looking
steadily at one place, said, " Why, it's Father.
Oh, he's so glad I'm coming." Nor was her
husband present at the time. Moreover the
sceptical reader is likely to deny the existence
of telepathy and would reject any explanation
based upon that ground.

The next case has reached me from America
and is a well authenticated instance on the
authority of a distinguished man, Dr. Minot J.
Savage, with whom I was acquainted. Dr.
Minot Savage was for many years a valued
member of our S.P.R., he died in 1920. Dr.
Hyslop [1] has recorded the following case in one

[1] As some of my readers may not be acquainted with
Dr. Hyslop's name, I may mention that he was for some
years the Professor of Ethics and Logic in Columbia
University, New York. He studied for some years in
Germany, where he took his Ph.D. and was also an LL.D.
He was at first a sceptic and severe critic of psychical
research, but afterwards became convinced of the importance of the subject, and resigned his university chair
and all its emoluments to devote the rest of his life to the
investigation of psychical phenomena. His zeal and
energy and acumen were remarkable, in fact he sacrificed
his life through the incessant labour involved in his duties
as treasurer, hon. secretary and research officer of the
American S.P.R. His literary output was enormous ;
he seemed to live and move and have his being in psychical
research to the exclusion of almost every other subject.
He spent some time with me in Ireland, and gave a learned
address to the recently founded Dublin Section of the
S.P.R. He died in 1920.

of his books [1] and remarks : " Dr. Savage told me personally of the facts and gave me the names and addresses of the persons on whose authority he tells the incidents," which Dr. Savage narrates, as follows :

" In a neighbouring city were two little girls, Jennie and Edith, one about eight years of age and the other but a little older. They were schoolmates and intimate friends. In June, 1889, both were taken ill of diphtheria. At noon on Wednesday Jennie died. Then the parents of Edith, and her physician as well, took particular pains to keep from her the fact that her little playmate was gone. They feared the effect of the knowledge on her own condition. To prove that they succeeded and that she did not know, it may be mentioned that on Saturday, June 8th, at noon, just before she became unconscious of all that was passing about her, she selected two of her photographs to be sent to Jennie, and also told her attendants to bid her good-bye.

" She died at half-past six o'clock on the evening of Saturday, June 8th. She had roused and bidden her friends good-bye, and was talking of dying, and seemed to have no fear. She appeared to see one and another of the friends she knew were dead. So far it was like other similar cases. But now suddenly, and with every appearance of surprise, she turned to her father and exclaimed, ' Why,

[1] " Psychical Research and the Resurrection " (Boston, U.S.A.), 1908, p. 88.

papa, I am going to take Jennie with me ! ' Then she added, ' Why, papa ! you did not tell me that Jennie was here ! ' And immediately she reached out her arms as if in welcome, and said, ' Oh, Jennie, I'm so glad you are here ! ' "

In connexion with this case Dr. Savage remarks that it is difficult to account for the incident by any ordinary theory of hallucination. If this vision were a solitary case, a mere casual coincidence might perhaps account for it, but as it is only one of a considerable group of similar cases an explanation of chance coincidence becomes incredible. My readers will doubtless agree with Dr. Savage's remark, as they peruse the other cases narrated in this volume.

The following case [1] was given in a paper contributed to the S.P.R. by Mr. Edmund Guruey and Mr. F. W. H. Myers.[2] It was received by them through the Rev. C. J. Taylor. The narrator, who does not wish his name published, was the Vicar of H—— :

" On November 2nd and 3rd, 1870, I lost my two eldest boys, David Edward and Harry, from scarlet fever, they being then three and four years old respectively.

[1] This case and the next one are quoted from pp. 99 and 100 respectively of the same book as the last. See footnote p. 18.

[2] " Proceedings S.P.R.," Vol. V, p. 459.

" Harry died at Abbot's Langley on November 2nd, fourteen miles from my vicarage at Aspley, David the following day at Aspley. About an hour before the death of this latter child he sat up in bed, and pointing to the bottom of the bed said distinctly, ' There is little Harry calling to me.' Of the truth of this fact I am sure, and it was heard also by the nurse.

" (Signed)   X.Z., Vicar of H—— "

In letters and conversations with Mr. Podmore, Mr. Taylor adds the following details : " Mr. Z. [the Vicar] tells me that care was taken to keep David from knowing that Harry was dead, and that he feels sure that David did not know it.   Mr. Z. was himself present and heard what the boy said.   The boy was not delirious at the time."

The next case was communicated to the S.P.R.[1] by the Rev. J. A. Macdonald, who has for some years been a useful helper to the Society in the careful collection of evidence. Mr. Macdonald received it at first hand from Miss Ogle, who was the sister of the percipient. She writes as follows :

" My brother, John Alkin Ogle, died at Leeds, July 17th, 1879.   About an hour before he expired he saw his brother—who had died about sixteen years before—and John, looking up with fixed

<hr />

[1] See " Proceedings S.P.R.," Vol. V, p. 460.

interest, said, ' Joe ! Joe ! ' and immediately after exclaimed with ardent surprise, ' George Hanley ! ' My mother, who had come from Melbourne, a distance of about forty miles, where George Hanley resided, was astonished at this, and said, ' How strange he should see George Hanley ; he died only ten days ago.' Then turning to my sister-in-law she asked if anybody had told John of George Hanley's death ; she said ' No one.' My mother was the *only* person present who was aware of the fact. I was present and witnessed this.

" (Signed) HARRIET H. OGLE "

In answer to inquiries, Miss Ogle states :

" J. A. Ogle was neither delirious nor unconscious when he uttered the words recorded. George Hanley was an acquaintance of John A. Ogle, not a particularly familiar friend. The death of Hanley was *not* mentioned in his hearing."

The " Revue Spirite " for December, 1924, contains the following interesting case :

" The Review ' Verdade e Luz ' of San Paolo, Brazil, in its number of September, 1924, has remarks on the striking incident of which the dying Adamina Lazaro was the heroine.

" A few hours before her death, the patient said to her father that she saw near her bed several members of the family, all deceased some years previously. The father attributed this declaration *in extremis* to a state of delirium, but Adamina insisted with renewed force, and among the invisible 'visitors' named her own brother, Alfredo, who was employed at the time at a distance of 423 kilometres, on the lighthouse of the port of Sisal.

" The father was more and more convinced of the imaginary nature of these visions, well knowing that his son Alfredo was in perfect health, for a few days previously he had sent the best possible news of himself.

" Adamina died the same evening, and the next morning her father received a telegram informing him of the death of the young Alfredo. A comparison of times showed that the dying girl was still living at the time of the death of her brother."

I am indebted to Mr. C. J. Hans Hamilton for the following case, which he translated from the Review " Psychica "[1] of 1921. It was contributed by M. Warcollier, of the Institut Metapsychique, Paris, who says :

" My uncle, M. Paul Durocq, left Paris in 1893 for a trip to America, with my aunt and other members of the family. While they were at Venezuela my uncle was seized with yellow fever, and he died at Caracas on the 24th June, 1894.

" Just before his death, and while surrounded by all his family, he had a prolonged delirium, during which he called out the names of certain friends left

[1] Published in France.

in France, and whom he seemed to see. 'Well, well, you too—, and you ——, you as well ! '

" Although struck by this incident, nobody attached any extraordinary importance to these words at the time they were uttered, but they acquired later on exceptional importance when the family found, on their return to Paris, the funeral invitation cards of the persons named by my uncle before his death, and who had died before him. It is only recently that I have been able to collect the testimony of the only two survivors of this event, my cousins Germaine and Maurice Durocq."

Germaine Durocq writes, as follows :

" You ask me details of the death of my poor father. I well remember him as he lay dying, though it is many years ago. The thing which probably interests you is that he told us of having seen some persons in heaven and of having spoken to them at some length. We were much astonished on returning to France to find the funeral cards of those same persons whom he had seen when dying. Maurice, who was older than I was, could give you more details on this subject."

Maurice Durocq writes :

" Concerning what you ask me with regard to the death of my father, which occurred a good many years ago, I recall that a few moments before his death my father called the name of one of his old companions—M. Etcheverry—with whom

he had not kept up any connexion, even by correspondence, for a long time past, crying out, ' Ah !
you too,' or some similar phrase. It was only on
returning home to Paris that we found the funeral
card of this gentleman. Perhaps my father may
have mentioned other names as well, but I do not
remember."

Mr. Hans Hamilton, who translated and sent
the above incident to me comments on it as
follows : " The date of the deaths of the
persons seen by M. Durocq when dying, should
have been verified at the time of the return of
the family to Paris, since we have otherwise no
certainty that they died before M. Durocq.
However, the whole of the story makes it more
than probable that this point would not have
been overlooked by the family ; and M. Warcollier states in his own account that the
persons in question were deceased at the time
of the apparitions."

The following incident was sent to the
" Spectator " by " H. Wedgwood " in 1882.
He says :

" Between forty and fifty years ago a young girl,
a near connexion of mine, was dying of consumption. She had lain for some days in a prostrate
condition taking no notice of anything, when she
opened her eyes, and looking upwards, said slowly,
' Susan—and Jane—and Ellen,' as if recognizing

the presence of her three sisters, who had previously died of the same disease. Then after a short pause she continued, ' and Edward too ! '—naming a brother then supposed to be alive and well in India—as if surprised at seeing him in the company. She said no more, and sank shortly afterwards. In the course of the post, letters came from India announcing the death of Edward, from an accident a week or two previous to the death of his sister.

" This was told to me by an elder sister who nursed the dying girl, and was present at her bedside at the time of the apparent vision." [1]

Miss Frances Power Cobbe, Authoress of " The Peak in Darien," recites an incident of a very striking character as having occurred in a family united very closely by affection :

" A dying lady, exhibiting the aspect of joyful surprise, spoke of seeing, one after another, three of her brothers who had been long dead, and then apparently recognized last of all a fourth brother, who was believed by the bystanders to be still living in India. The coupling of his name with that of his dead brothers excited such awe and horror in the mind of one of the persons present that she rushed from the room. In due course of time letters were received announcing the death of the brother in India, which had occurred some time before his dying sister seemed to recognize him." [2]

[1] See R. Pike's " Life's Borderland and Beyond," p. 29.
[2] *Ibid.*, p. 18.

Dr. E. H. Plumptre (the Dean of Wells), writing to the " Spectator," August 26 1882, remarks :

" The mother of one of the foremost thinkers and theologians of our time was lying on her death-bed in the April of 1854. She had been for some days in a state of almost complete unconsciousness. A short time before her death, the words came from her lips, ' There they are, all of them—William and Elizabeth, and Emma and Anne ' ; then, after a pause, ' and Priscilla too.' William was a son who had died in infancy, and whose name had never for years passed the mother's lips. Priscilla had died two days before, but her death, though known to the family, had not been reported to her."[1]

In connexion with the subject of this chapter the case of Mrs. Z. in Chapter V, p. 102, should also be read.

---

[1] See R. Pike's " Life's Borderland and Beyond," p. 15.

CHAPTER III

VISIONS SEEN BY THE DYING OF PERSONS KNOWN BY THEM TO BE DEAD, AND DEATH-BED VISIONS SEEN BY OTHERS

" I believe no soul is left to wing its viewless flight to Paradise in solitude. I believe the ' Gloria in Excelsis ' of the shining host of God welcomes the disembodied spirit upon the confines of the new world. I remember hearing once of a little dying child shrinking timidly from the idea of going alone ; but just before the end there came a spirit of sublime confidence, a supernatural opening of vision, a recognition of some companionship, and the little one cried out : ' I am not afraid ; they are all here.' . . . I believe the chamber of the dying is filled with the holy angels."
—BASIL WILBERFORCE

THERE are a great many records authenticated by those who have attended the last moments of a dying friend or patient, wherein shortly before death an ecstatic vision seems to have been granted to the dying person, whose face lights up with joy and apparent recognition of some relative before he passes into the Unseen. It is needless to quote a great number of cases, as doubtless many of my readers will be familiar with instances. Such cases are not confined to one country or one nation, but they appear to be more or less common all over the world. Here for instance is a case which occurred amongst the Cree Indians of Saskatchewan :

The Assistant Matron of the Ahtahkakoops Indian Hospital, Sandy Lake Reserve, Saskatchewan, Canada, writes to me on January 28, 1925, about a patient in the hospital, as follows :

" He was a Cree Indian lad, about 20 years of age, son of Chief Papewyn, of a neighbouring Reserve. He was in the last stage of phthisis and had been brought here to be cared for till the finish. He was placed in a wigwam about a 100 yards distant.

" At last the supreme day arrived. It was evening and I was with him. He was lying quietly in his bed when suddenly he sat up, stretched forth his arms with a yearning gesture, while an ecstatic smile broke over his face. It was not simply a smile of pleasure, but something far beyond it. The veil was lifted, and no one who was looking on could fail to realize that it was a glorious vision that met his gaze. He then lay back in his bed, looked at me with a smile, and passed away. He had been calm and collected during the day, there was no delirium ; it was an unclouded glimpse of that higher life into which he was just entering.

" (Signed)   R. HUTCHINSON
" *Assistant Matron* "

Some interesting cases of visions seen by dying persons are given in a little book by Mrs. Joy Snell,[1] who was a nurse in a large hospital, and the cases she narrates are her own personal experiences, and not narratives related at second-hand. Mrs. Snell seems to be a careful and conscientious recorder, and she has kindly furnished me with the names and other particulars of the cases given anonymously in her book.

I quote below a few of these cases as given by her :

"I recall the death of a woman (Mrs. Brown, aged 36) who was the victim of that most dreadful disease, malignant cancer. Her sufferings were excruciating, and she prayed earnestly that death might speedily come to her and end her agony. Suddenly her sufferings appeared to cease ; the expression of her face, which a moment before had been distorted by pain, changed to one of radiant joy. Gazing upwards, with a glad light in her eyes, she raised her hands and exclaimed, ' Oh, mother dear, you have come to take me home. I am so glad ! ' And in another moment her physical life had ceased.

"The memory of another death which occurred about the same time comes back to me. It was that of an old soldier (Mr. Auchterlonie, aged 59) who was in the last stages of tuberculosis brought

[1] " The Ministry of Angels."

on by exposure while fighting his country's battles. He was brave and patient but had frequent paroxysms of pain that were almost unendurable, and he longed for the relief which he knew death alone could bring him. One of these spasms had seized upon him, and his features were convulsed with agony as he fought for breath, when he suddenly grew calm. A smile lit up his face, and looking upwards he exclaimed, with a ring of joy in his voice, 'Marion, my daughter!' Then the end came. His brother and sister were at the bedside. The sister said to the brother, 'He saw Marion, his favourite daughter. She came and took him where he will suffer no more.' And she added fervently, 'Thank God! he has found rest at last.'"

In Chapter VI other cases related by Mrs. Snell will be found.

Miss R. Canton, of Garway Road, London, W., sends me the following case, which I quote in her own words, as follows:

"Some years ago I went to see a cousin of mine at Acton, who was very ill, and I was told by her sister that on the previous evening as she sat down on a chair by the bedside, the invalid exclaimed, 'Oh, don't J—! Oh, you have sent Mother away, she was sitting there!' and she continued to seem much distressed. My aunt had died some years previously. The dying girl told me about this herself when we were alone."

The following is a case of Vision of the
Dying, translated from " La Revue Spirite "
for January, 1925.

" Mr. A. R. Besancon writes as follows :

" ' At the commencement of February, 1915, at
M——, when I was only ten years old, I had the
grief of losing my mother. Her death was accompanied by circumstances which I take the liberty
of relating. My mother was attended by my
grandmother during her illness. One night the
latter was surprised at hearing my mother, who
was sleeping in the next room, pronounce certain
sentences, among others this :—" Marie, I can see
you at last, I am glad you have come. Help me."
(Marie was my sister who died a few years before
this.) Grandmother thought it was a dream ; she
rose and approached my mother's bed, and to her
great surprise she found her in a perfectly normal
state. My mother even told her the satisfaction
she had had in seeing her daughter. Later on in
the night the " conversation " was resumed, but
we paid no further attention. But on the next
morning, Mother was no more.

" ' Moreover, during the same night, one of my
aunts who lived in the neighbouring village of
V——, had the clear impression of seeing mother.
" She passed," she said to me the following day,
" beside my bed without speaking, then went to
embrace my two daughters and disappeared."
Such are the facts.' "

The following case is quoted from Mr.

Richard Pike's "Life's Borderland and Beyond" (p. 46) :

"In the summer of 1883, a young man named Giles, of Nottingham, had the misfortune to lose several children after long and painful periods of illness. The two eldest, Fred and Annie, aged respectively seven and eight, had died and been buried for some weeks when his little boy of four years old showed symptoms of approaching death.

"The father and mother were constantly by his side, as will be readily believed, to mitigate the little fellow's sufferings as much as possible. On the night when he died the father came to his bedside with the customary medicine, when the little boy, sitting upright in bed, cried out : 'There's Fred and Annie.' 'Where, my boy ?' asked the father. 'Don't you see them there—there ?' said the lad, pointing to the wall, 'they're waiting for me to go to them,' and the next minute the little sufferer fell back on the pillow dead. It should be mentioned that the father saw nothing of the apparition to which his dying boy so vividly pointed, but he quite believes its reality."

Mrs. Kinloch, of Boundary Road, St. John's Wood, N.W., sends me instances of Visions of the Dying, which had been told her, and which I quote in her words :

"My sister—who has recently passed over—who was with our mother when she died, told me that on the day before her death she suddenly called out, 'Oh, look at your father over there,' and pointed to a corner of the room, but my sister could see nothing.

" A poor woman whom I knew told me the other day that just before her mother died, she said suddenly, ' Tom, bring the boat nearer ; I can't get in.' ' Tom ' was her husband."

In this case, and the next three cases, the apparitions seem to have had a more or less premonitory purpose. The incident was related to the editor of the review " Psychica," who considered it so interesting that she requested the lady to repeat it by letter, which she willingly did, only requesting that nothing more than her initials should be published, though her name and address were known to the editor of the review.

The letter is as follows :

" DEAR MADAM,
" With reference to the incident I related to you, which happened several years ago, the following are the facts just as they occurred :
" I lost my daughter when she was seventeen years of age ; she had been ill for some five years, and for eight months before her death had been confined to her bed. During all this time, and up to her death, she maintained a remarkable degree of intelligence and will. A fortnight before her

death, one evening when I was leaning over the head of her bed, I asked her what she was thinking of, seeing her absorbed. She replied, 'Little mother, look there,' pointing to the bed-curtains. I followed the direction of her hand and saw a man's form, completely white, standing out quite clearly against the dark curtain. Having no ideas of spiritism, my emotion was intense, and I closed my eyes not wishing to see any longer. My child said to me, ' You do not reply.' I had the weakness to declare to her, ' I see nothing ' ; but my trembling voice betrayed me doubtless, for the child added with an air of reproach, ' Oh, little mother, I have seen the same thing for the last three days at the same hour ; it's my dear father who has come to fetch me.'

" My child died 15 days later, but the apparition was not repeated ; perhaps it attained its greatest intensity on the day I saw it.

" (Signed) Z. G."

The editor of " Psychica " remarks : " The lady who signs this letter is not a credulous person, and she declares that she saw the vision near the bed of her dying child at a time when her thoughts were far from the creation of a phantasmal form.

" Carita Borderieux "
(*Editor of " Psychica "*)

Mr. Hans Hamilton, who translated the above extract, remarks : " The interest of this case lies in the fact of the apparition having taken place 15 days before death ; in its being visible to two persons ; and in the fact that there is not the least suspicion of either delirium or coma on the part of the dying girl."

A striking case of *collective hallucination* (that is to say, a vision seen by the relatives of the dying person as well as by the dying person herself) is given in the " Proceedings S.P.R." for 1889.[1]

The narrator, Miss Emma Pearson, writes an account of her aunt's illness and death, which is here given considerably abridged :

" My aunt, Miss Harriet Pearson, who was taken very ill at Brighton in November, 1864, craved to be back in her own home in London, where she and her sister Ann (who had died some years previously) had spent practically all their lives. I accordingly made the necessary arrangements, and had her moved home. Her two nieces (Mrs. Coppinger and Mrs. John Pearson), Eliza Quinton the housekeeper, and myself did the nursing between us. She became worse and worse. On the night of Dec. 23rd Mrs. John Pearson was sitting up with her, while Mrs. Coppinger and I lay down in the adjoining room, leaving the door ajar to hear any sound from the next room. We were neither of us asleep, and suddenly we both started up in bed,

[1] See " Proceedings S.P.R.," Vol. VI, p. 20. Also " Human Personality," Vol. II, p. 334.

as we saw someone pass the door, wrapped up in an old shawl, having a wig with three curls each side, and an old black cap. Mrs. Coppinger called to me, ' Emma, get up, it is old Aunt Ann ! ' I said, ' So it is ; then Aunt Harriet will die to-day ! ' As we jumped up, Mrs. John Pearson came rushing out of Aunt Harriet's room, saying, ' That was old Aunt Ann. Where has she gone ? ' I said to soothe her, ' Perhaps it was Eliza come down to see how her old mistress is.' Mrs. Coppinger ran upstairs and found Eliza asleep. Every room was searched —no one was there ; and from that day to this no explanation has ever been given of this appearance, except that it was old Aunt Ann come to call her sister. Aunt Harriet died at 6 p.m. that day."

Eliza Quinton, the housekeeper, confirms the above statement, and adds : " We searched in every room but could not find anyone in the house. Miss Harriet died on the evening of that day, but before that she told us all that she had seen her sister, and that she had come to call her."

This last statement is further confirmed by Miss Emma Pearson in a later letter, in which she states that she remembers her Aunt saying that " her sister had come for her, for she had seen her."

In the following case the premonitory purpose seems to be strongly marked :

Louise F., aged forty-eight, died after an abdominal operation in January, 1896. During her illness she frequently asked that, when cured, she might take her little niece Lily, aged three years and three months, of whom she was very fond, to live with her in the country. About a month after the death of her aunt little Lily, who was intelligent and precocious and in quite good health, often stopped in her play to look fixedly out of the window. Her mother asked her what she was looking at, and she answered, "It is Aunt Louise, who holds out her arms to me and calls me." Her mother, much frightened, tried to distract her attention, but the child drew her chair to the window and continued to look for several minutes. Her brother, M. F., who gave me these details, said, "I was then eleven years old and my little sister said, 'What! Don't you see Tata?' as she called her aunt. Of course I could see nothing." For some months nothing further was seen by the child, the visions ceased. Towards May 20th, little Lily fell ill, and when in bed she looked up to the ceiling saying that she saw her aunt calling her, surrounded by little angels. "Mother, how pretty!" she said. From day to day her illness increased, but she always repeated, "My aunt has come to fetch me ; she is holding out her arms to me," and as her mother wept, she said, "Don't cry, Mother, it is very beautiful, there are angels round me." She died on the 9th of June of tubercular meningitis, four and a half months after the death of Louise F.

Such is the story told by her brother, M. F., confirmed by his sister, G. F., and her mother. The family lived very quietly in a country town. None of them know anything of psychic science.

The following case was first printed in the "Religio-Philosophical Journal," May 5, 1894.[1] Mr. B. B. Kingsbury, who contributed it, states that the informant is a member of the Presbyterian Church, and her husband confirmed her statement of voices heard by the little boy calling him. Mr. Kingsbury adds that both his informants, Mr. and Mrs. H., are worthy of the highest credit. The father is somewhat of a "sensitive," and the mother has had two or three clairvoyant experiences herself.

The statement just as it was given by the mother runs as follows:

"Had I ever doubted that there is a life beyond, my doubt would have been removed by what I call a vision. In 1883 I was the mother of two strong, healthy boys. The eldest was a bright boy of two years and seven months. The other a darling baby boy of eight months. August 6th, 1883, my baby died. Ray, my little son, was then in perfect health. Every day after baby's death (and I may safely say every hour in the day) he would say to me, 'Mamma, baby calls Ray.' He would often leave his play and come running to me, saying, 'Mamma, baby calls Ray all the time.' Every

[1] See "Human Personality," Vol. II, p. 334.

night he would waken me out of my sleep and say, ' Mamma, baby calls Ray all the time. He wants Ray to come where he is ; you must not cry when Ray goes, Mamma ; you must not cry, for baby wants Ray.' One day I was sweeping the sitting- room floor, and he came running as fast as he could run, through the dining-room where stood the table with baby's high chair (which Ray now used) at the side. I never saw him so excited, and he grabbed my dress and pulled me to the dining-room door, jerked it open, saying, ' Oh, Mamma, Mamma, come quick ; baby is sitting in his high chair.' As soon as he opened the door and looked at the chair, he said, ' Oh, Mamma, why didn't you hurry ; now he's gone ; he laughed at Ray when he passed the chair ; oh, he laughed at Ray so nice. Ray is going with baby, but you must not cry, Mamma.' Ray soon became very sick. Nursing and medicine were of no avail. He died Oct. 13th, 1883, two months and seven days after baby's death. He was a child of high intelligence and matured far beyond his years. Whether it is possible for the dead to return, and whether my baby came back and was seen by his little brother or not, we leave for others to judge."

Dr. Hodgson, whose name is well known to all psychical researchers as one of the most careful and critical investigators, made in- quiries regarding the case, and in reply to Dr. Hodgson's inquiries, Mrs. H. wrote :

" DEFIANCE, OHIO
" *December* 13*th*, 1894

" When the child ran to me telling me the baby was sitting in his chair at the table, there was no one in the house but the servant girl, little Ray, and myself. I told the girl nothing about it and she did not hear the child, but as soon as my husband came to dinner I told him. After that we talked freely of the matter to several of our friends Little Ray knew nothing of death ; we had never spoken of it to him in any way ; the last time I took him to the baby's grave, shortly before he was taken sick, we were sitting by the grave, and I thought, ' Oh, if I could only take baby up and look at it for just one minute, I would feel so glad.' *Instantly* Ray said to me, ' Mamma, let us take baby up and look at it just one minute ; then we will feel better.'   Just as we were leaving the grave he smoothed it with his little hand, and said, ' Ray is going to lie down and sleep right here beside little brother, but you must not cry, Mamma.'   He is now lying just where he said he would.

P.S.—I wish to say that I have never known much of what is called modern Spiritualism, but was born and reared a Presbyterian and still belong to that Church, of which I am an active member.

" F. H."

Dr. Hodgson also wrote to Mr. H., who replied as follows :

" *Feb.* 27*th*, 1895

" I can truly say that my wife related it [that is,

about Ray seeing baby in the chair] to me the day it occurred when I came to dinner. I frequently heard our little boy tell his mamma that the baby called him all the time.

"W. H. H."

The following corroboration was also received by Dr. Hodgson :

"116 SUMMIT STREET
"DEFIANCE, OHIO
"*Feb. 25th,* 1895

"DEAR SIR,
"I can truly say that Mrs. and Mr. H. often spoke to me of Ray seeing the baby in the chair before he took sick. They told me the next day after it happened.

"(Mrs.) J. H. SHULTERS"

The following case was given by Dr. Paul Edwards, and was published in the Journal "Light" for April, 1906 :

"While living in a country town in California (U.S.A.) about the year 1887, I was called upon to visit a very dear lady friend who was very low and weak from consumption. Every one knew that this pure and noble wife and mother was doomed to die, and at last she herself became convinced that immediate death was inevitable, and accordingly she prepared for the event. Calling her children to her bedside she kissed each in turn, sending them away as soon as good-bye was said. Then came the husband's turn to step up and bid farewell to a most loving wife, who was perfectly clear in her mind. She began by saying ' Newton ' (for that was his Christian name) . . . 'do not weep over me, for I am without pain and am wholly serene. I love you upon earth, and shall love you after I have gone. I am fully resolved to come to you if such a thing is possible, and if it is not possible I will watch you and the children from Heaven, where I will be waiting when you all come. My first desire now is to go. . . . I see people moving—all in white. The music is strangely enchanting. Oh ! here is Sadie ; she is with me—and—she knows who I am.' Sadie was a little girl she had lost about ten years before. ' Sissy ! ' said the husband, ' you are out of your mind.' ' Oh, dear ! why did you call me here again ? ' said the wife, ' now it will be hard for me to go away again ; I was so pleased while there— it was so delightful—so soothing.' In about three minutes the dying woman added, ' I am going away again and will not come back to you even if you call me.'

" This scene lasted for about eight minutes, and it was very plain that the dying wife was in full view of the two worlds at the same time, for she described how the moving figures looked in the world beyond, as she directed her words to mortals in this world.

" . . . I think that of all my death scenes this was the most impressive—the most solemn."

My friend Miss Dallas has sent me some cases of Visions of the Dying which occurred to persons she knew.

In one case the face of her friend's mother, just before death, suddenly lighted up with an intense brilliancy. When this had passed away, the dying woman opened her eyes and said that she had looked into Heaven, and had seen many people they knew who had passed over, and also that many of the things she had seen it was impossible to describe. Shortly after this she died.

In another case Miss Dallas tells of a widow, living with her youngest surviving son, Jim, then dying of consumption. Miss Dallas visited the mother shortly after her son's death, and recorded the following in her note-book the same day :

" Jim had died on a Thursday, and on the previous Sunday his end appeared to be near, but he revived, and told his mother that he had seen something beautiful. Again he had a relapse, and on reviving he said he had seen two of his sisters and a brother who had died previously, but he added, ' Mother, I cannot find Bessie.' His mother told Miss Dallas that Bessie had died twelve years before, when Jim was still a child. Not long after this Jim died."

The following case is taken from the Journal

of the American S.P.R. for July, 1909 (p. 422). The editor, Prof. Hyslop, relates how the original letter came into his possession, and remarks that it may be taken as documentary evidence of the incident narrated. The original letter was enclosed in one addressed to the editor of the " Open Court," a well-known American periodical. In it the writer, Mr. William C. Church, states that the letter he forwards was written to the late Captain J. Ericsson, inventor of the Monitor, by Lady Ellen Chute, a relative of his wife, and concerns the death of Ericsson's sister-in-law, Louisa Browning. The "Amelia" referred to in the letter was the wife of Captain Ericsson, who had died in July, 1867, many years previously ; and " Aunt Louisa Browning " was the sister of " Amelia."

" BRACKNELL, BERKS
" *November 5th*, 1883

" DEAR CAPT. ERICSSON,

' " Since I last wrote to you our fond aunt, Louisa Browning, died on Sunday morning, October 28th, at the age of 78.   On her death-bed she appeared to see her deeply loved sister [Capt. Ericsson's wife, Amelia], who had gone before.   Those watching by her heard her say—though she had before been quite unconscious—' Oh, Amelia ! Amelia ! ' and she reached out her hand to welcome someone their earthly eyes were not permitted to see, and then all was over. . . .

" Yours very sincerely,

" (Signed) ELLEN CHUTE "

In the case [1] here abridged, the singing and voice of the unseen visitant were heard by the mother as well as by her dying child ; and a cousin of the deceased child appears to have had a vision of the child and heard a premonitory intimation of her death.

" Mrs. G., with her two little girls, Minnie and Ada, of the respective ages of eight and nine years, had been staying in the country on a visit to her sister-in-law, but having taken a house near London, she sent the two children with their nurse off by an early train, following herself by one a few hours later. Towards the evening of the same day, one of the little girls walked into the room of the house which they had quitted in the morning, where a cousin to whom she was much attached was sitting at his studies, and said to him, ' I am come to say good-bye, Walter ; I shall never see you again.' Then kissing him she vanished from the room. The young man was greatly startled and astonished, as he had himself seen both the little girls and their nurse off by the morning train.

" At this very time of the evening both the

[1] See R. Pike's " Life's Borderland and Beyond," p. 28, in which the " Atlantic Monthly," of March, 1879 is quoted as the source.

children in London were taken suddenly ill, while playing in their new home, a few hours after they had arrived. The doctor called in pronounced their complaint to be small-pox of the most malignant kind. They both died within the week, but the youngest, Minnie, died first. The day after she was buried, the poor bereaved mother was anxiously watching the last hours of the one still left, for whom she well knew no chance of life remained. Suddenly the sick child woke up from a kind of stupor, and exclaimed, ' Oh, look, Mamma, look at the beautiful angels ! ' pointing to the foot of the bed. Mrs. G. saw nothing, but heard soft sweet music, which seemed to float in the air. Again the child exclaimed : ' Oh, dear Mamma, there is Minnie ! She has come for me ' ; she smiled and appeared greatly pleased. At this moment Mrs. G. distinctly heard a voice say, ' Come, dear Ada, I am waiting for you ! ' The sick child smiled once again and died without a struggle.''

Some time before their death the poor mother overheard a childish conversation between the two little ones, in which the youngest, Minnie, said to the other that she felt sure she should die first, and would be certain to come and fetch her sister. This conversation was long remembered by the mother, as it was strikingly confirmed by the actual facts. It is, of course, possible that expectancy on the part of the mother (if at the time she recalled her children's conversation) may discount the evidential value of this striking case.

It has been recorded of the celebrated mathematician, Prof. De Morgan, that during the last two days of his life there were indications of his passing through the experience which he had himself considered worthy of investigation and of record. He seemed to recognize all those of his family whom he had lost—his three children, his mother and sister, whom he greeted, naming them in the reverse order to that in which they left the world. No one seeing him at that moment could doubt that what he seemed to perceive was, to him at least, visible and real.[1]

Mrs. De Morgan in her book, " From Matter to Spirit," relates the following incident, which she gives as it was told by the mother of the dying child.

" On the morning on which John died, having bade all the family farewell, he lay for some time quite quiet, and then he spoke, his voice sounding strong and clear, and was evidently replying to some question which he had heard asked. We were astonished and awestruck. We felt that he

[1] See R. Pike's " Life's Borderland and Beyond," p. 15.

saw and heard an angel invisible to us. Then he spoke again and said, ' Mother, here is Grandmother come ! You must see her ! And she is with such a great company, and they say that they are come to take me away with them.' Soon after that he gently breathed his last." [1]

The Rev. W. G. Horder relates the following incident, and says :

" A friend of mine, of a mind naturally indisposed to faith, and at the time quite sceptical about a future life, tells me of the following incident, which made a deep impression upon him, and even wakened belief in immortality :

" His brother, a young man of about 25 years of age, had been seized with brain fever, which at last rendered him quite unconscious for about 24 hours, but just before death he raised himself in his bed, resting himself upon his hand and said, ' Who is that at the bottom of my bed ? ' His mother, who was sitting by his bedside, said, ' There is no one there, my dear.' He said, ' Don't you see Emma ' (a departed sister) ' standing at the foot of the bed ? ' She said, ' No, there is no one there, my dear.' ' Yes, there is,' he said, ' it is Emma. I am coming, I am ready'; and fell back and died." [2]

The following three cases were sent to me by Mrs. Shepherd Munn, widow of the late Vicar

[1] See Mrs. De Morgan's " From Matter to Spirit," p. 184.

[2] See R. Pike's " Life's Borderland and Beyond," p. 35.

of Orleton, Brimfield, Herefordshire, to whom
all the people concerned in the narratives were
known personally. She writes as follows :

" A young boy, aged fourteen, named Charles
Dyer, who lived with his parents at Orleton, was
dying of consumption, and had wasted away very
rapidly in four or five months. During the whole
of that period he was very bright, full of interest in
all around, and did not seem to be aware of his
rapidly failing strength. About a week before he
died he slept in a room off his mother's, with no
door between—he called her, and when she went
in, he was full of excitement about a door he could
see at the corner of his room, which he said was
' opening wider and wider, and when it is open wide
I shall be going through it, Mother.'

" On the morning of the day he died, his mother
having left the room to fetch him something, heard
him call and hastening back, found him sitting up
in bed, looking towards the corner of the room, and
he said to her, ' There is a nice old man come for
me ; he is holding out his arms for me.   I must
go.   Don't fret, Mother ' ; and he fell back gently
on his pillow and was gone, without any struggle
for breath, and with a smile of joy on his face,
which remained.

" His mother was full of ecstasy, and came down
to the Vicarage that same morning to tell me of it.
The impression this experience made upon her has
continued to the present day, and has influenced
her life for the better."

The following case, also related to me by Mrs. Shepherd Munn, took place some years previous to the last, but is connected with the same family.

" An old man, named John George—grandfather of the consumptive boy, Charles Dyer, already referred to—lay dying. He and his wife, Mary Ann George, had had a great sorrow that same year in the death of their youngest son, Tom, a young man who had been killed on the railway line on which he worked.

" The dying man had been quiet for some time as though sleeping, when he suddenly looked up, opened his eyes wide, and looking at the side of the bed opposite to where his wife was, exclaimed, ' Why, Mother, here is Tom, and he is all right, no marks on him. Oh, he looks fine.' Then after another silence he said, ' And here's Nance too.' A pause, then ' Mother, she is all right. She has been forgiven.' And very soon after he passed away, taking with him a sorrow which had long pressed upon the mother's heart, for Nance had fallen into sin, and had died soon after the child was born, and as the poor mother thought ' never having had time to repent.' "

The next case is also given by Mrs. Shepherd Munn, and it also, like the two preceding cases, occurred in Orleton, Herefordshire.

" A woman, named Mary Wilding, was dying of cancer. She was passionately fond of her husband,

Charles Wilding. They had worked together, brought up their children, saved some money, and bought a nice little house in Orleton, where they spent some comfortable and happy years together. When she realized that she would die and leave ' Charlie,' she became very unhappy and made them all very miserable by fretting and constantly complaining of her fate.

" One day as the end drew near, when a sister of hers, who was helping to look after her, happened to be alone in the room with Mary Wilding, she suddenly looked up with such a bright expression of face and said, ' Oh, Emmie, Mother is here ; she has come for me, and is going to take me with her.' She never lost the feeling of confidential joy, and passed away the day after quite peacefully."

Dr. .Hyslop narrates the following case, which he received from a friend whose testimony he had no reason to question :

" I called this afternoon (May 14th, 1906) upon a lady whose child, a boy of nine years old, had died two weeks previously. He had been operated upon for appendicitis some two or three years ago, and had had peritonitis at the same time. He recovered and was apparently quite well for a time. Again he was taken ill, and was taken to hospital and operated upon. He was perfectly rational, recognizing his parents, the doctor and the nurse —after recovering from under the influence of the anæsthetic. Feeling that he was going, he asked his mother to hold his hands until he should be gone. Soon he looked up and said, ' Mother, dear, don't you see little sister over there ? ' ' No, where is she ? ' ' Right over there. She is looking at me.' Then the mother to pacify him said she saw the child. In a few minutes his face lighted up full of smiles, and he said, ' There comes Mrs. C.' (a lady of whom he was very fond, who had died nearly two years before), ' and she is smiling just as she used to. She is smiling and wants me to come.' In a few moments he said, ' There is Roy ! I'm going to them. I don't want to leave you, but you'll come to me soon, won't you ? Open the door and let them in. They are waiting outside,' and he was gone."

The mother confirms this narrative, and inquiry brings out the following facts. The " little sister " he refers to had died four years before his own birth. " Roy " is the name of a friend of the child, who had died about a year previous.

The following case is taken from the " Life of the Rev. Dwight L. Moody," the celebrated Evangelical preacher of the United States. The last moments of Mr. Moody are described by his son, the biographer, as follows :

"Suddenly he murmured, ' Earth recedes, heaven opens up before me. I have been beyond the gates. God is calling. Don't call me back. It is beautiful. It is like a trance. If this is death it is sweet.'

" Then his face lit up and he said in a voice of joyful rapture, ' Dwight ! Irene ! I see the children's faces ' (referring to his two little grandchildren, who had gone before). Turning to his wife he said, ' Mamma, you have been a good wife to me,' and with that he became unconscious."

The following case is related by Mr. Alfred Smedley in his book of " Reminiscences " (pp. 50, 51). He gives an account of his wife's last moments, and states :

" A short time before her decease, her eyes being fixed on something that seemed to fill her with pleasant surprise, she exclaimed, ' Why ! there is sister Charlotte here, and Mother and Father, and brother John and sister Mary ! And now they have brought Bessie Heap ! ! They are all here. Oh ! how beautiful ! Cannot you see them ? ' she asked. ' No, my dear ; I very much wish I could,' I answered. ' Cannot you see them ? ' she again asked in surprise ; ' why they are all here, and they are come to bear me away with them ! ' Then she added, ' Part of our family have crossed the flood, and soon the other part will be gathered home, and then we shall be a family complete in heaven ! '

" I may explain here that Bessie Heap had been the trusted family nurse, and my wife had always been a favourite with her.

" After the above ecstatic experience my wife lingered for some time. Then fixing her gaze steadily upward again, and lifting up her hands, she joined the convoy of angel friends, who had come to usher her into that brighter spiritual world of which we had learned so little."

The next case [1] is given on the authority of Dr. Wilson of New York, who was present at the death a few years ago of the well-known American tenor, Mr. James Moore, who was a patient of his. Dr. Wilson gives the following narrative :

" It was about four o'clock, and the dawn for which he had been watching was creeping in through the shutters, when, as I bent over the bed, I noticed that his face was quite calm and his eyes clear. The poor fellow looked up into my face, and taking my hand in both of his, he said, ' You've been a good friend to me, Doctor. You've stood by me.' Then something which I shall never forget to my dying day happened, something which is utterly indescribable. While he appeared perfectly rational and as sane as any man I have ever seen, the only way that I can express it is that he was transported into another world, and although I cannot satisfactorily explain the matter to myself, I am fully convinced that he had entered the Golden City—for he said in a stronger voice than he had used since I had attended him, ' There is Mother ! Why, Mother, have you come here to see me ? No, no, I'm coming to see you. Just wait, Mother, I am almost over. I can jump it. Wait, Mother.' On his face there was a look of inexpressible

[1] See " Psychical Research and the Resurrection." J. H. Hyslop. Boston, U.S.A., 1908, p. 97.

happiness, and the way in which he said the words impressed me as I have never been before, and I am as firmly convinced that he saw and talked with his mother as I am that I am sitting here.

" In order to preserve what I believed to be his conversation with his mother, and also to have a record of the strangest happening of my life, I immediately wrote down every word he had said. . . . His was one of the most beautiful deaths I have ever seen."

My friend, Mrs. Carter, of St. Erth, Hayle, Cornwall, sends me the following case, which occurred on April 13, 1924, when she was present, and she wrote the following notes a few days later. She says :

" On Sunday, April 13th, I went to Hillside to sit with a Mr. Williams, who was dying of consumption, so that those belonging to him might have a little rest. He was in a state of great physical distress, and unable to lie down, and could only breathe with the greatest difficulty, with his head leaning down to within a few inches of the mattress.

" He suddenly raised himself and stretched out his hands, and said very clearly, as though speaking to someone present and whom he was glad to see, ' Edmund ! ! my dear brother Edmund ! ! ' I was alone with him at the time, but when the family returned to the room later I at once related to them what he had said, and then learnt from them that his brother Edmund was dead.

" During the time that I was with him—from 3.15 to 9.15—although breathing very heavily all the time, he appeared to be quite conscious when he spoke, and called for the different members of his family. He knew me quite well, and kissed my hand and called me by my name. He also asked to have water at intervals, and asked for hot tea. In spite of his great bodily distress, his trust in God remained quite unshaken, and it was very moving to hear him say at intervals, ' Dear Lord, let me go ! '

" I was told that before I arrived he had exclaimed, ' Mrs. Hooper ! ' She had been a great friend of his, and died here about 18 months or two years ago. He died about ten hours after I had left."

The following account of the last days of a little child was published in the " Journal of the American S.P.R.," edited by Dr. James H. Hyslop (Vol. XII, No. 6), and a considerably abridged report was compiled by Miss H. A. Dallas,[1] a summary of which is given below :

" Daisy Irene Dryden was born in Marysvill, Yuba County, California, on September 9th, 1854. She died in San José, California, on October 8th, 1864, aged ten years and twenty-nine days.

" Her mother writes : ' In the summer of 1864 Daisy was attacked by bilious fever. After five weeks of illness the fever left her, and for two weeks

[1] See " The Nurseries of Heaven," Vale Owen and Dallas. London, 1920, p. 117.

she seemed to continue to gain strength. She smiled and sang and seemed like herself again, until one afternoon, as her father sat by her bed, he noticed a singular expression on her face. It was one of both pleasure and amazement. Her eyes were directed to one place above the door Her father asked, "Daisy, what is it? What do you see?" She replied softly, "It is a spirit, it is Jesus. And He says I am going to be one of His little lambs." "Yes, dear," said her father, "I hope you are one of His Lambs." "Oh, papa!" she exclaimed, "I am going to heaven, to Him."

"'That night she was taken with enteritis and only lived four days. She suffered much for the first twenty-four hours, being unable to retain food, water, or medicine. From that time on she had very little pain. Her poor little body had in fact become so attenuated that there was little left for the disease to work upon. But her mind was very active and remarkably clear. Her faculties appeared sharpened. She could remember recitations she had learned in school, always having been fond of memorizing poetry. And when Lulu sang to her from the Sunday School Hymnal, she would give the name of the song and the page on which to find it.

"'She loved to have us read the Scriptures to her. I read, in John xiv, "It is expedient for you that I go away: for if I go not away the Comforter will not come unto you, but if I depart I will send Him unto you." At this she looked up to me so heavenly as she said, "Mamma, when I go away the Comforter will come to you ; and maybe He will let me come too sometimes ; I'll ask Allie about it." She often said this after this time, when she felt uncertain about anything. Allie was her brother who had passed to the other life at the age of six, of scarlet fever, seven months before. He seemed to be with her a great deal of the time during those last three days, because when we asked her questions which she could not answer she would say, " Wait till Allie comes, and I will ask him." On this occasion she waited only a short time and then said, " Allie says I may go to you sometimes ; he says it is possible, but you will not know when I am there ; but I can speak to your thought."

" 'As I have said, Daisy lingered on the border-land for three days, after the first agonizing twenty-four hours had passed. Her physical frame had become so emaciated that there was only enough to hold the spirit in its feeble embrace ; and it was manifested to us, as it were, through the thin veil of the attenuated flesh which enwrapped it. During this time she dwelt in both worlds, as she expressed it. Two days before she left us, the Sunday School Superintendent came to see her. She talked very freely about going, and sent a message by him to the Sunday School. When he was about to leave, he said, " Well, Daisy, you will soon be over the ' dark river.' " After he had gone, she asked her father what he meant by the " dark river." He tried to explain it, but she said, " It is all a mistake ; there is no river ; there is no curtain ; there is not even a line that separates this life from the other life." And she stretched out her little hands from the bed, and with a gesture said, " It is here and it is there ; I know it is so, for I can see you all, and I see them there at the same time." We asked her to tell us something of that other world and how it looked to her, but she said, " I cannot describe it ; it is so different, I could not make you understand."

" ' One morning while I was in the room, putting it in order, Mrs. W., one of our kind neighbours, was reading to her these words from the Testament : " Let not your heart be troubled. In my Father's house are many mansions. I go to prepare a place for you " (John xiv, 1, 2). Daisy remarked, " Mansions, that means houses. I don't see real houses there ; but there is what would be places to meet each other in. Allie speaks of going to such and such a place, but says nothing of houses. You see, perhaps the Testament tells about mansions so we will feel we are going to have a home in heaven, and perhaps when I get there I'll find a home. And if I do, the heavenly flowers and trees that I love so much here—for I do see them, and that they are more beautiful than anything you could imagine—they will be there." I said, " Daisy, don't you know the Bible speaks of heaven being a beautiful city ? " She said, " I do not see a city," and a puzzled look came over her face, and she said, " I do not know ; I may have to go there first."

" ' Mrs. W., a kind neighbour, the one who had

read of the mansions to Daisy, and who was with us a great deal, told Mrs. B., a neighbour of hers, about Daisy's inner sight being open. Mrs. B. was a lady who did not believe in a future state. She was, moreover, in deep distress, having just lost her husband and a son who was about twelve years old, named Bateman. She came with Mrs. W. one evening, and, sitting beside the bed, began to ask questions. Daisy said to her : " Bateman is here, and says he is alive and well, and is in such a good place, he would not come home for anything. He says he is learning how to be good." Mrs. B. then said, " Ask him if he has seen his father." Daisy replied, " He says he has not, he is not here, and says to you, ' Mother, don't fret about me, it is better I did not grow up.' " This communication set the mother to thinking and she became a firm believer in a future state.

" ' The following morning, when alone with Daisy, Mrs. W., who had brought Mrs. B. to see her, asked Daisy how she could think Mrs. B.'s son was happy. " For," said she, " when he was here, you know he was such a bad boy. Don't you remember how he used to swear, and steal your playthings, and break them up ? You know we did not allow him to play with you nor with my children, because he was so bad." Daisy replied, " Oh, Aunty, don't you know he never went to Sunday School, and was always hearing so much swearing ? God knows he did not have half a chance."

" ' The same day her Sunday School teacher

Mrs. H., who also was with her a great deal, was sitting beside her, when Daisy said to her, " Your two children are here." Now, these children had gone to the other life several years before, and if they had lived in this world would have been nearly grown up. Daisy had never heard anyone speak of them, nor did the mother have any pictures of them, so she could not have known anything whatever about them before seeing them in the spiritual world. When asked to describe them, her description of them as full-grown did not agree with the mother's idea of them, so she said, " How can that be ? They were children when they died." Daisy answered, " Allie says, ' Children do not stay children ; they grow up as they do in this life.' " Mrs. H. then said, " But my little daughter Mary fell, and was so injured that she could not stand straight." To this Daisy replied, " She is all right now ; she is straight and beautiful ; and your son is looking so noble and happy."

" ' Once she said : " Oh, papa, do you hear that ? It is the singing of the angels. Why, you ought to hear it, for the room is full of it, and I can see them, there are so many ; I can see them miles and miles away."

" ' Mrs. W., already mentioned, who had lost her father a short time previous, wanted to know if Daisy had seen him, and brought his picture to let her see if she could recognize him. But in the evening, when she came again, Daisy told her she had not seen him, and that Allie, whom she had asked about him, had not seen him, but that Allie had said he would ask someone who could tell him about him. In a moment Daisy said, "Allie is here and says, 'Tell Aunty her father wants her to meet him in heaven, for he is there.' Mrs. W. then said, "Daisy, why did not Allie know at once about my father?" "Because," replied she, "those who die go into different states or places and do not see each other at all times, but all the good are in the state of the blest."

"'During those last days of illness Daisy loved to listen to her sister Lulu as she sang for her, mostly from the Sunday School song-book. Lulu sang one song, the chorus of which was:

> "'Oh! come angel band,
> Come and around me stand,
> Oh! bear me away on your snowy wings
> To my immortal home.

When she had finished, Daisy exclaimed, "Oh, Lulu, is it not strange? We always thought the angels had wings! But it is a mistake; they don't have any." Lulu replied, "But they must have wings, else how do they fly down from heaven?" "Oh, but they don't fly," she answered, "they just come. When I think of Allie, he is here."

"'Once I inquired, "How do you see the angels?" She replied, "I do not see them all the time; but when I do, the walls seem to go away, and I can see ever so far, and you couldn't begin to count the people; some are near, and I know them; others I have never seen before." She mentioned the name of Mary C., the sister of Mrs. S., who was a neighbour of ours in Nevada City, and said, " You know she had such a bad cough, but she is well now, and so beautiful, and she is smiling to me."

" ' I was then sitting beside her bedside, her hand clasped in mine. Looking up so wistfully to me, she said, " Dear Mamma, I do wish you could see Allie ; he is standing beside you." Involuntarily I looked round, but Daisy thereupon continued, " He says you cannot see him because your spirit-eyes are closed, but that I can, because my body only holds my spirit, as it were, by a thread of life." I then inquired, " Does he say that now ? " " Yes, just now," she answered. Then wondering how she could be conversing with her brother when I saw not the least sign of conversation, I said, " Daisy, how do you speak to Allie ? I do not hear you or see your lips move." She smilingly replied, " We just talk with our think." I then asked her further, " Daisy, how does Allie appear to you ? Does he seem to wear clothes ? " She answered, " Oh, no, not clothes such as we wear. There seems to be about him a white, beautiful something, so fine and thin and glistening, and oh, so white, and yet there is not a fold, or a sign of a thread in it, so it cannot be cloth. But makes him look so lovely." Her father then quoted from the Psalmist : " He is clothed with light as a garment." " Oh, yes, that's it," she replied.

" ' She often spoke of dying, and seemed to have such a vivid sense of her future life and happiness

that the dread of death was all dispelled. The
mystery of the soul's departure was to her no
more a mystery. It was only a continuation of
life, a growing up from the conditions of earth-life
into the air and sunshine of heaven.

" ' The morning of the day she died she asked me
to let her have a small mirror. I hesitated, thinking the sight of her emaciated face would be a
shock to her. But her father, sitting by her,
remarked, " Let her look at her poor little face if
she wants to." So I gave it to her. Taking the
glass in her two hands, she looked at her image for
a time, calmly and sadly. At length she said,
" This body of mine is about worn out. It is like
that old dress of Mamma's hanging there in the
closet. She doesn't wear it any more, and I won't
wear my body any more, because I have a new
spiritual body which will take its place. Indeed, I
have it now, for it is with my spiritual eyes I see
the heavenly world while my body is still here.
You will lay my body in the grave because I will
not need it again. It was made for my life here,
and now my life here is at an end, and this poor
body will be laid away, and I shall have a beautiful
body like Allie's." Then she said to me, " Mamma,
open the shutters and let me look out at the world
for the last time. Before another morning I shall
be gone." As I obeyed her loving request, she
said to her father, " Raise me up, Papa." Then,
supported by her father, she looked through the
window whose shutters I had opened, and called
out, " Good-bye, sky. Good-bye, trees. Good-bye,

flowers. Good-bye, white rose.   Good-bye, red
rose.   Good-bye, beautiful world," and added,
" how I love it, but I do not wish to stay."

" ' That evening, when it was half-past eight,
she herself observed the time, and remarked, " It
is half-past eight now ; when it is half-past eleven
Allie will come for me."   She was then, for the
time being, reclining on her father's breast,
with her head upon his shoulder.   This was a
favourite position, as it rested her.   She said,
" Papa, I want to die here.   When the time comes,
I will tell you."

" ' Lulu had been singing for her, and as half-
past eight was Lulu's bedtime she arose to go.
Bending over Daisy, as she always did, she kissed
her, and said, " Good night."   Daisy put up her
hand and, stroking tenderly her sister's face, said
to her, " Good night."   When Lulu was half-way
up the stairs, Daisy again called out after her, in a
clear, sweet, earnest tone, " Good night and good-
bye, my sweet, darling Lulu."

" ' At about a quarter past eleven she said,
" Now, Papa, take me up ; Allie has come for me."
After her father had taken her, she asked us to
sing.   Presently someone said, " Call Lulu," but
Daisy answered promptly, " Don't disturb her, she
is asleep," and then, just as the hands of the clock
pointed to the half-hour past eleven, the time she
had predicted that Allie was to come to take her
with him, she lifted up both arms and said, " Come,
Allie," and breathed no more.   Then tenderly
laying her loved but lifeless form upon the pillow,

her father said, " The dear child has gone," and added, " she will suffer no more." ' "

There are one or two specially interesting points about this case—like Case I in Chapter II —the dying child kept a consciousness of the visions which came to her, together with clear recognition of her earthly friends, and ability to converse with them sensibly. With Daisy Dryden the double consciousness lasted a few days, whereas in the case of Mrs. B. it only lasted an hour or two.

Again the descriptions Daisy gave of her vision evidently did not accord with her pre-conceived ideas of a spiritual world, yet it did not once occur to her to doubt the reality of what she was learning of a life apart from a material body—and the possession of a spiritual body.

In p. 118 of " The Nurseries of Heaven " (see p. 56 above) is the following statement made by her mother : " Although she was on the whole a good child, possessing ordinary good sense, yet in no way was she more remark-able than many other children. Her dying experience, therefore, was not the outgrowth of a life highly spiritual, nor was it one which had been educated in the least degree on the lines of mysticism or modern spiritualism."

Her father was so deeply impressed " by

what she most undoubtedly said, heard and revealed to them," that he began a careful study of the New Testament in the original Greek, and published a series of articles later on the subject.[1]

The following incident taken from the " American S.P.R. Journal " for 1918 (Vol XII, p. 623), was reported by Dr. E. H. Pratt, of Chicago :

" My sister Hattie, while attending school at Mt. Carroll Seminary, suffered an attack of malignant diphtheria. She was brought home to be under our father's care, but he was unable to save her, and after a few days of extreme suffering her spirit took its flight into what seems to most of us such a dark, impenetrable expanse of appalling immensity. A death-bed scene occurred, so wonderful, realistic, and impressive, that although I was but ten years of age at the time, my memory picture of that event is as vivid and distinct as though it were taken but yesterday.

" Her bed was in the middle of the living-room, and my mother, father, younger sister, and a few friends were standing about it, gazing earnestly upon my sister's dear features, as the light of life gradually went out, and the ashy pallor of death settled over them. Hattie's going out was not abrupt. It was a gradual fading away, very calm

[1] " Resurrection of the Dead," published by Hitchcock and Walden, Cincinnati, in 1872.

and apparently free from pain. Although her throat was so choked up with diphtheritic membrane that her voice was very thick, and it required close attention to catch all of her words, her mind seemed unusually clear and rational.

" She knew she was passing away, and was telling our mother how to dispose of her little personal belongings among her close friends and playmates, when she suddenly raised her eyes as though gazing at the ceiling toward the farther side of the room, and after looking steadily and apparently listening for a short time, slightly bowed her head, and said, ' Yes, Grandma, I am coming, only wait just a little while, please.' Our father asked her, ' Hattie, do you see your grandma?' Seemingly surprised at the question she promptly answered, ' Yes, Papa, can't you see her? She is right there waiting for me.' At the same time she pointed toward the ceiling in the direction in which she had been gazing. Again addressing the vision she evidently had of her grandmother, she scowled 'a little impatiently and said, ' Yes, Grandma, I'm coming, but wait a minute, please.' She then turned once more to her mother, and finished telling her what of her personal treasures to give to different ones of her acquaintances. At last giving her attention once more to her grandma, who was apparently urging her to come at once, she bade each of us good-bye. Her voice was very feeble and faint, but the look in her eyes as she glanced briefly at each one of us was as lifelike and intelligent as it could be. She then fixed her eyes steadily on her vision but so faintly that we could but just catch her words, said, ' Yes, Grandma, I'm coming now.' Then without a struggle or evidence of pain of any kind she gazed steadily in the direction she had pointed out to us where she saw her grandma, until the absence of oxygen in her blood-stream, because respiration had ceased, left her hands and face all covered with the pallor of lifeless flesh.

" She was so clear-headed, so positive of the vision and presence of her grandma, with whom she talked so naturally, so surprised that the rest of us could not see grandma, the alternation of her attention and conversation between her grandma and father and mother were so distinctly photographed upon the camera of my brain that I have never since been able to question the evidence of the continuance of distinct recognizable life after death. Her grandmother had died a few years previously, and before that she and grandma had always been such close friends, and the recognition of each other as Hattie left her body to join her dearly beloved grandma in the realms beyond the vision of our physical eyes was so unquestionable and complete in every detail that it seems impossible to account for the remarkable event on any theory except that her grandma was alive and so completely like herself while on earth that Hattie's recognition of her was instantaneous and unquestionable, a real genuine experience."

The following case was communicated to the

American S.P.R. by Mr. S. B. Bennett (see " American S.P.R. Journal " for 1918, Vol. XII, p. 607) :

" PITTSTON, PA.,
" *December* 15, 1906

" Mr. G. H. Tench died in 1902, after years of patient though intense suffering of cancer. He lived in Wilkes-Barre, but was formerly a near neighbour of mine in West Pittston, during a portion of the time he was a foreman under me enjoying mutual confidence and esteem. He received deserved promotion by another Coal Co., but our personal relation remained the same.

" During the last weeks I watched with him as often as I could, going back and forth by rail. While suffering intensely he would not take narcotics nor stimulating medicine, saying, ' I have lived Hall Tench and I am going to die that way.' The night the end came he roused his younger son, telling him to call the family as he was going away. He talked entirely rationally to them and was fully conscious. Later a brother came to the house and upon entering the room G. H. Tench said, ' Good-bye, Will ; I am going soon,' and closed his eyes. The family thought the end had come, but after a short interval he opened his eyes and, looking over and above the bed foot, with raised head and every appearance of interest, said clearly and distinctly, ' Why, they're all plain people.' This closed the scene, which was described to me by his wife soon after the funeral.

" Now Tench was not a religious man, although attended by a Methodist minister at the last, but a moral, upright man in every relation of life, thoroughly courageous, as was shown by his refusal to have his sensibilities dulled in his suffering. Not highly educated, nor a great reader, yet I have no doubt he had thought about conditions he had to face, and was *likely* to have imbibed the wings and harp idea. Is it not possible that he at the last expressed surprise that the people waiting for him should be ' all plain people ' ? I give you this as a *fact*.

" (Signed) S. B. BENNETT "

The following narrative was recorded in the " Journal of the American Society for Psychical Research " (1918, p. 603), having been sent to Prof. Hyslop by Mr. Rud. C. Gittermann, a member of the English S.P.R. He writes as follows :

" My father died in Germany on March 18th, 1892, and my mother then came to live with us at Odessa. Shortly after she fell ill, and died on May 6th of the following year, 1893. Both she and my father had always been most sceptical of anything concerning the existence and survival of the soul.

" A few minutes before her death she regained consciousness (having been in a state of coma for two hours previously), raised herself in her bed, stretched out her arms, and with a happy smile on her face, cried out, ' Papa ! Papa ! ' just as if she suddenly saw him in front of her. Immediately after she fell back into the arms of my wife, and expired.

" My mother used to call her husband ' Papa,' just as we children did.

" I certify that this is a perfectly true account of what took place.

" (Signed) RUD. C. GITTERMANN "

The following abridged account of the last days of the American poet, Horace Traubel, is taken from a fuller narrative in the American S.P.R. " Journal " for 1921 (Vol. XV, pp. 114-123).

Horace Traubel (1858-1919) was the Boswell of Walt Whitman ; he was also author of a number of volumes of poems of the Whitman type, which some of his own disciples regard as equalling those of his master. He was also the founder of the well-known Contemporary Club of Philadelphia.

The abridged account was contributed by Mrs. Flora Macdonald Denison, who was present at the death-bed, to the April-May issue of a Magazine entitled, " The Sunset of Bon Echo," as follows :

" All day on August 28th Horace was very low spirited. Anne's illness and the going of the Bains was too much for him. Mildred was with him a good deal and we decided not to leave him a minute. He had been brought in from the veranda but absolutely radiant, and on seeing me, he called out, ' Look, look, Flora, quick, quick, he is going.' ' What, Horace,' I said, ' what do you see ? I cannot see anyone.' ' Why just over the rock Walt appeared, head and shoulders and hat on in a golden glory—brilliant and splendid. He reassured me—beckoned to me, and spoke to me. I heard his voice but did not understand all he said, only " Come on." '

" Frank Bain soon came in and he repeated the story to him. All the rest of the evening Horace was uplifted and happy. So often Horace would say, ' Do not despise me for my weakness,' but now he was quite confident, even jocular, as I handed him a drink.

" On the night of September 3rd Horace was very low. I stayed for a few hours with him. Once his eyes rolled ; I thought he was dying, but he just wanted me to turn him. As I did so, he listened and seemed to hear something. Then he said, ' I hear Walt's voice, he is talking to me.' I said, ' What does he say ? ' He said, ' Walt says, " Come on, come on." ' After a time he said, ' Flora, I see them all about me, Bob and Bucke and Walt and the rest.'

" Colonel Cosgrave had been with Horace in the afternoon and had seen Walt on the opposite side of the bed, and felt his presence. Then Walt passed through the bed and touched the Colonel's hand, which was in his pocket. The contact was like an electric shock. Horace was also aware of Walt's visible presence and said so. There was no gloom about the house. No one seemed depressed. A feeling of triumph, of pride, and of exultation permeated the atmosphere."

A letter was afterwards received by Mr. Walter Prince of the American S.P.R., from Col. Cosgrave, confirming the statement given by Mrs. Flora Denison as above.

There are several cases of which records have been preserved in the " Proceedings " of the Society for Psychical Research and elsewhere, in which an account is given of those watching beside a dying relative having had a vision of spirit forms near the bed.

" In one case [1] two women watching by their dying sister, Charlotte, saw a bright light and within it two young faces hovering over the bed, gazing intently at Charlotte; the elder sister recognized these faces as being two of her brothers, William and John, who had died when she was young. The two sisters continued to watch the faces till they gradually ' faded away like a washed-out picture,' and shortly afterwards their sister Charlotte died."

Mr. Podmore, who investigated this case, remarks that it is possible the vision was due to a telepathic impact from the dying person,

[1] See " Proceedings S.P.R.," Vol. VI, p. 293.

but this explanation is less tenable and quite as unlikely as is the percipience of spirit forms by the dying person and sometimes by those present. Mr. Podmore, with his usual prejudice against any supernormal explanation remarks on this that " the images traditionally associated with death receive a sensory embodiment," but this point of view is not appropriate to the two following cases where the percipients being very young children could hardly be supposed to have any mental images traditionally associated with death, nor does it account for the " collective hallucination " described in Miss Pearson's case, pp. 35, 36.

This case is quoted by Stainton Moses :

" Miss H., the daughter of an English clergyman, was tending a dying child. His little brother, aged three to four years, was in a bed in the same room. As the former was dying, the little brother woke up, and, pointing to the ceiling with every expression of joy, said, ' Mother, look at the beautiful ladies round my brother ! How lovely they are, they want to take him.' The child died at that moment."

Another instance is reported by M. Pelusi, librarian at the Victor Emmanuel Library at Rome (Luce e Ombra, 1920, 20) :

" A little girl of three, Hippolyte Notari, partly paralysed, was in the same room with her little brother of four months, who was dying. The father, the mother, and the grandmother of the two children were present. About fifteen minutes before the death of the infant, little Hippolyte stretched out her arms, saying, ' Look, mother, Aunt Olga.' This Aunt Olga was a younger sister of Mme. Notari, who had killed herself a year previously owing to a disappointment in love. The parents asked, ' Where do you see Aunt Olga ? ' The child said, ' There, there ! ' and tried insistently to get out of bed to go to her aunt. They let her get up, she ran to an empty chair and was much discountenanced because the vision had moved to another part of the room. The child turned round and said, pointing to a corner, ' Aunt Olga is there.' Then she became quiet and the baby died."

In the following case which was communicated by Prof. W. C. Crosby, Associate Member, Society for Psychical Research [" Proceedings S.P.R.," Vol. VIII, pp. 229–231] the vision was seen by the nurse during the unconsciousness of the dying patient. The phantom seen was unknown to the percipient.

" Mrs. Caroline Rogers, seventy-two years old, a widow who had been twice married, and whose first husband, a Mr. Tisdale, died about thirty-five years ago, has lived on Ashland Street, in Roslindale, Mass., for the last twenty-five years ; and since the death of her last child some years ago she has lived quite alone. Early in March of this year she was stricken with paralysis, and after an illness of nearly six weeks died on the afternoon of Tuesday, April 15th.

" Mrs. Mary Wilson, a professional nurse, forty-five years old, attended Mrs. Rogers during her illness, remaining with her almost constantly until she died. She had never seen Mrs. Rogers before the latter's illness, and knew nothing of her family or history. Mrs. Rogers spoke frequently to Mrs. Wilson, and also to others, as had long been her custom, of her second husband, Mr. Rogers, and children, expressing a desire to see them again, etc.

" On the afternoon of April 14th, Mrs. Rogers became unconscious, and remained so all the time until her death twenty-four hours later. Mrs. Wilson sat up with her through the whole of Monday night. Mrs. Wilson's daughter Ida, twenty-five years old, kept her mother company, and a boy of ten or twelve years slept in an adjoining chamber, to be called in case of an emergency. These four were the only persons in the house. The outer doors were securely locked, the door leading from the sick chamber on the second floor into the hall was kept locked all the time because it was near the foot of Mrs. Rogers' bed ; and entrance to the sick chamber was gained by passing from the upper hall into the living-room by a door which was locked that night, and thence through the chamber in which the boy slept—the two chambers having been made to communicate by cutting a door through the back of a small closet. This door was diagonally facing the bed on which Mrs. Rogers lay. Mrs. Wilson rested on a settee placed at right angles to the head of Mrs. R.'s bed, so that when lying down her face was almost directly opposite this door and not more than ten or twelve feet from it. The lamp, which burned brightly all night, stood on a small table in the corner of the room directly opposite the door ; and Ida occupied a couch against the wall and between the lamp and door.

" Mrs. Wilson was pretty well worn out with her long vigil ; believing that Mrs. Rogers was dying, she was naturally very nervous and timid ; and having heard Mrs. R. speak frequently of seeing her departed friends, etc., she had a feeling of expectancy and dread with regard to supernatural visitations. Between two and three a.m., while her daughter was asleep, and while she was resting on the settee, but wide awake, she happened to look toward the door into the adjoining chamber and saw a man standing exactly in the doorway, the door being kept open all the time. He was middle-sized, broad-shouldered, with shoulders thrown back, had a florid complexion, reddish-brown hair (bareheaded) and beard, and wore a brown sack overcoat, which was unbuttoned. His expression was grave, neither stern nor pleasant, and he seemed to look straight at Mrs. Wilson, and then at Mrs. Rogers without moving. Mrs. Wilson supposed, of course, that it was a real man, tried to think how he could have got into the house. Then, as he remained quite motionless, she began to realize that it was something uncanny, and becoming frightened, turned her head away and called her daughter, who was still asleep on the couch, awakening her. On looking back at the door after an interval of a minute or two the apparition had disappeared ; both its coming and going were noiseless, and Mrs. Rogers remained perfectly quiet, and so far as could be known entirely unconscious during this time. The chamber into which this door leads being quite dark, there was no opportunity to observe whether or not the apparition was transparent. Mrs. Wilson shortly afterwards went into this chamber and the living-room, but did not examine the lower part of the house until morning, when the doors were found properly locked and everything all right.

"In the morning Mrs. Rogers' niece, Mrs. Hildreth, who lives in the neighbourhood, and has known Mrs. R. and her family for many years, called at the house. Mrs. Wilson related her experience to her and asked if the apparition resembled Mr. Rogers, and Mrs. Hildreth replied emphatically that it did not. (All who knew Mr. Rogers are agreed on this point.) Their conversation was interrupted then, but when resumed later in the day Mrs. Hildreth said that Mrs. Wilson's description agreed exactly with Mr. Tidsale, Mrs. Rogers' first husband. Mrs. Rogers came to Roslindale after marrying Mr. Rogers, and Mrs. Hildreth is the only person in that vicinity who ever saw Mr. Tisdale ; and in Mrs. Rogers' house there is no portrait of him nor anything suggestive of his personal appearance. Mrs. Wilson is also very positive that the apparition was unlike anyone she ever knew.

" Mrs. Wilson has had similar experiences before, and at least one, which occurred when she was eighteen years old, which appears to have been veridical.

" The foregoing account of my experience is correct in every particular.

" (Signed)   MARY WILSON "

" The foregoing is a full and accurate statement of Mrs. Wilson's experience as she related it to me on the morning of April 15th.

" (Signed)   F. E. HILDRETH "

June 5th, 1890

" Mrs. Wilson and Mrs. Hildreth have both impressed me as being intelligent and perfectly honest and truthful ; and I have no doubt that Mrs. Wilson's experience was real and substantially as she has described it.

" (Signed)   W. O. CROSBY "

CHAPTER IV

VISIONS SEEN BY THE DYING OF LIVING PERSONS AT A DISTANCE—IN SOME CASES RECIPROCAL

WE now come to a somewhat different and large class of cases where the veil which hides the spiritual world is not for a few moments lifted for the dying percipients, but their souls appear to be transported to a different place *on earth* and they are able to see persons who may be at a remote distance. Such cases are usually called instances of " travelling clairvoyance " and numerous well-attested facts of this kind have been collected in " Phantasms of the Living," to which my readers are referred.

There are, however, a few cases which are worthy of special notice, wherein the dying persons appear not only to make themselves visible at a distance, but also inform those around them where they have been, and that they have visited those whom they desired to see.

One of the most remarkable and pathetic of these so-called " reciprocal cases " was related to me by that gifted and venerable Quaker lady, Miss Anna Maria Fox, when we were on a voyage to Canada for the British Association Meeting in 1884. Miss Fox and her sister Caroline were well known to *savants* in the last generation,[1] for their beautiful place " Penjerrick," near Falmouth in Cornwall, was the rendezvous of many eminent scientific and literary men, and nearly fifty years ago I had the privilege of enjoying their hospitality. When narrating the incident, Miss Fox referred me to her relatives, the Birkbecks, for confirmation of it : and this was given me when I made inquiries shortly afterwards.

Mr. Myers has given an abridged record of the same case,[2] which he obtained from another member of the same family, Mrs. Charles Fox of Falmouth, who had heard the account from one of the percipients.

The incident is nearly two centuries old, but as Mr. Myers says, the Fox family is one which would carefully preserve evidence of this kind. As an illustration of this fact I may state that the narrative which Miss Anna Maria Fox gave me was practically identical with that given by Mrs. Charles Fox, which I now quote :

" In 1739 Mrs. Birkbeck, wife of William Birkbeck, banker, of Settle, and a member of the Society of Friends, was taken ill and died at

[1] See " Memoirs of Caroline Fox."
[2] See " Phantasms of the Living," Vol. II, p. 560.

Cockermouth, while returning from a journey to Scotland, which she had undertaken alone—her husband and three children, aged seven, five, and four years respectively, remaining at Settle. The friends at whose house the death occurred made notes of every circumstance attending Mrs. Birkbeck's last hours, so that the accuracy of the several statements as to time, as well as place, was beyond the doubtfulness of man's memory, or of any even unconscious attempt to bring them into agreement with each other.

" One morning, between seven and eight o'clock, the relation to whom the care of the children at Settle had been entrusted, and who kept a minute journal of all that concerned them, went into their bedroom as usual, and found them all sitting up in their beds in great excitement and delight. Mamma has been here ! ' they cried, and the little one said, ' She called " Come, Esther ! " ' ' Nothing could make them doubt the fact, and it was carefully noted down, to entertain the mother on her return home. That same morning, as their mother lay on her dying bed at Cockermouth, she said, ' I should be ready to go if I could but see my children.' She then closed her eyes, to reopen them, as they thought, no more. But after ten minutes of perfect stillness she looked up brightly and said, ' I am ready now ; I have been with my children ' ; and then at once peacefully passed away. When the notes taken at the two places were compared, the day, hour, and minutes were the same.

" One of the three children was my grandmother, *née* Sarah Birkbeck, afterwards the wife of Dr. Fell, of Ulverston. From her lips I heard the above almost literally as I have repeated it. The eldest was Morris Birkbeck, afterwards of Guildford. Both these lived to old age, and retained to the last so solemn and reverential a remembrance of the circumstance that they rarely would speak of it. Esther, the youngest, died soon after. Her brother and sister heard the child say that her mother called her, but could not speak with any certainty of having themselves heard the words, nor were sensible of more than their mother's standing there and looking on them."

The case of Mrs. Goffe is also of remote date, 1691, but is taken from a contemporary report made by the Rev. T. Tilson in a letter he addressed to the famous divine, Richard Baxter, who published it in a book he wrote.[1] The case is given in " Phantasms of the Living " (Vol. II, pp. 558, 559) and the authors state that the narrative cannot be impugned on the ground of any credulity on the part of Baxter, and quote an authority on this point. It will be seen that the incidents in the following narrative are curiously parallel to the preceding case of Mrs. Birkbeck. Though Mr. Tilson's letter which we now quote, is somewhat

[1] See Baxter's " The World of Spirits " (1691), pp. 147–51.

long, it is better to give his own words rather than an abstract.

"*July 6th,* 1691

"Mary, the wife of John Goffe, of Rochester, being afflicted with a long illness, removed to her father's house at West Mulling, which was about nine miles distant from her own ; there she died, June 4th, 1691. The day before her departure she grew impatiently desirous to see her two children, whom she had left at home, to the care of a nurse. She prayed her husband to hire a horse, for she must go home to die with her children.

"Between one and two o'clock in the morning she fell into a trance. One widow Turner, who watched with her that night, says that her eyes were open and fixed, and her jaw fallen ; she put her hand on her mouth and nostrils, but could perceive no breath ; she thought her to be in a fit, and doubted whether she was alive or dead. The next day this dying woman told her mother that she had been at home with her children. ' That is impossible,' said the mother, ' for you have been here in bed all the while.' ' Yes,' replied the other, ' but I was with them last night while I was asleep.'

"The nurse at Rochester, widow Alexander by name, affirms and says she will take her oath of it before a magistrate, and receive the sacrament upon it, that a little before two o'clock that morning she saw the likeness of the said Mary Goffe come out of the next chamber (where the elder child lay in a bed by itself, the door being left open), and stood by her bedside for about a quarter of an hour ; the younger child was there lying by her ; her eyes moved, and her mouth went, but she said nothing. The nurse, moreover, says that she was perfectly awake ; it was then daylight, being one of the longest days in the year. She sat up in her bed, and looked steadfastly upon the apparition ; at that time she heard the bridge clock strike two, and a while after said, ' In the name of the Father, Son, and Holy Ghost, what art thou ? ' Thereupon the appearance removed and went away ; she slipped on her clothes and followed, but what became of it she cannot tell. Then, and not before, she began to be grieviously affrighted, and went out of doors, and walked upon the wharf (the house is just by the river-side) for some hours, only going in now and then to look at the children. At five o'clock she went to a neighbour's and knocked at the door, but they would not rise ; at six she went again, then they rose and let her in. She related to them all that had passed ; they would persuade her she was mistaken, or dreamt ; but she confidently affirmed, ' If ever I saw her in all my life, I saw her this night.' " [The writer than gives an account of how one of those to whom she related the story confirmed the above narrative.]

" The substance of this statement was related to me by John Carpenter, the father of the deceased, the next day after the burial—July 2. I fully discoursed the matter with the nurse and two neighbours, to whose house she went that morning.

Two days after I had it from the mother, the minister that was with her in the evening, and the woman who sat up with her last that night. They all agree in the same story, and every one helps to strengthen the other's testimony. They all appear to be sober, intelligent persons, far enough off from designing to impose a cheat upon the world, or to manage a lie ; and what temptation they should lie under for so doing I cannot conceive.

" (Signed) THOMAS TILSON "

The next case, also contributed by Mr. Myers, is an account given by the Ellis family to Mr. Myers, of a vision which their father, Mr. Ellis, who was dying in Kensington, had of his son, Robert, at that time in Australia. The Misses Ellis state :

" On Wednesday, December 29th, 1869, my father, who was dangerously ill at the time, awoke from a sleep, and raising himself up in the bed pointed and looked most intently to one corner of the room and said to us (my sister Mary and me), ' Look ! don't you see ? it is my poor boy Bob's head ! ' Then turning to me, he said, ' Norman Town, don't forget, Gulf of Carpentaria.' He then sank back exhausted. This happened about three p.m. We found, after his death, he had entered the address in red ink in his pocket-book—my brother having left Bourke Town and gone to Norman Town—so that the next packet of letters were sent there. My father died on Thursday, Dec. 30th,

1869. When my brother returned from Australia a few years after, he told us that one night, whilst camping out, he had gone to rest and had slept, and he awoke seeing my father's head distinctly in one part of his tent. It made such an impression on him that he went to his mate in the adjoining tent and said, ' I have seen my father ; you must come and stay with me.' By the next mail he received my letter telling him of my father's death.

" My brother said it must have been about three a.m. when he saw my father. Would not that correspond with our three p.m. ? I always think they must have seen each other at the same time.

" (Signed) ALICE ELLIS
" MARY ELLIS "

Mr. Myers states that in conversation with the narrators, he ascertained that Mr. Ellis was not in the least delirious during his last days, and that he was deeply attached to his absent son.

In this case in connexion with the Vision of his father seen by Mr. Robert Ellis, it may be interesting to note that another case of apparition, occurring to her husband some years later, is given by Mrs. Robert Ellis. She states that on *Tuesday, December* 19, 1876, between 6 and 7 p.m., when she and Mr. Ellis were sitting talking together, he suddenly looked over his shoulder with a startled, almost terrified look, and on being asked what was the matter, he said that he had imagined he saw someone coming in at the door. Subsequently he stated that he distinctly saw the tall dark figure of a man, but could not distinguish his features. He was greatly agitated. Later on a telegram was received, giving news of the sudden death of Mrs. Robert Ellis' brother in Mexico on *Tuesday*, the 19*th December*, at seven o'clock in the evening. He and Mr. Robert Ellis had been very great friends.

This case is taken from " Phantasms of the Living," Vol. II, p. 253 :

" The lady who sends us the following narrative occupies a position of great responsibility, and desires that her name may not be published, but it may be given to inquirers :

" ' When I was eight months old, my mother's youngest sister, Mercy Cox, came to reside with us and to take charge of me. My father's position at the Belgian Court as portrait painter obliged him to be much abroad, and I was left almost wholly to the care of my very beautiful aunt. The affection that subsisted between us amounted almost to idolatry, and my poor mother wept many bitter tears when she came home to see how little I cared for anyone else. My aunt took cold, and for three years lingered in decline. I was a quick child and could read well and even play prettily, so that I was her constant companion day and night. Our doctor, Mr. Field, of the Charter House, greatly disapproved of this close contact, and urged my parents to send me quite away. This was a difficult feat to accomplish, the bare mention of the thing throwing my aunt into faintings. At last Mr. Cumberland (the theatrical publisher) suggested that I should join his two daughters, Caroline, aged 16, and Lavinia, younger, at Mrs. Hewetson's, the widow of a clergyman resident at Stourpaine, in Dorsetshire, who only took four young ladies. This was represented to my aunt as something so wonderfully nice and advantageous to me that she consented to part with me. My portrait was painted and placed by her bed, and I remember how constantly she talked to me about our separation. She knew she would be dead before the year of my absence would be ended. She talked to me of this, and of how soon I should forget her ; but she vehemently protested that she would come to me there. Sometimes it was to be as an apple-woman for me to buy fruit of, sometimes as a maid wanting a place, always *she* would know *me*, but I should not know her, till I cried and implored to know her.

" ' I was but nine when they sent me away, and coach travelling was very slow in those days. Letters too were dear, and I very rarely had one. My parents had sickness and troubles, and they believed the reports that I was well and happy, but I was a very miserable, ill-treated little girl. One morning at break of day—it was New Year's Day —I was sleeping beside Lavinia. We two shared one little white tester bed with curtains, while Caroline—upon whom I looked with awe, she being 16, slept in another similar bed at the other end of a long, narrow room, the beds being placed so that the feet faced each other, and two white curtains hung down at the sides of the head. This New Year's morning I was roughly waked by Lavinia shaking me and exclaiming, " Oh, look there ! There's your aunt in bed with Caroline." Seeing two persons asleep in the bed I jumped out and ran to the right side of it. There lay my aunt, a little on her right side, fast asleep, with her mouth a little open. I recognized her worked nightgown and cap. I stood bewildered, with a childish sort of wonder as to when she could have come ; it must have been after I went to bed at night. Lavinia's cries awakened Caroline, who as soon as she could understand, caught the curtains on each side and pulled them together over her. I tore them open, but only Caroline lay there, almost fainting from fright. This lady, Miss Cumberland, afterwards became Mrs. Part, wife of a celebrated doctor at Camden Terrace [and now deceased].

" ' I never talked of what had occurred, but one day after I had returned home, I said to my mother, "Do you know, Mamma, I saw Auntie when I was at school." This led to an explanation, but my mother instead of commenting upon it, went and fetched her mother saying to her, " Listen to what this child says." Young as I was I saw they were greatly shocked, but they would tell me nothing except that when I was older I should know all. The day came when I learned that my dear aunt suffered dreadfully from the noise of St. Bride's bells, ringing in the New Year. My father tried to get them stopped but could not. Towards morning she became insensible ; my mother and grandmother seated on either side of her and holding her hands, she awoke and said to my mother, " Now I shall die happy, Anna, I háve seen my dear child." They were her last words.

" ' (Signed)   D. E. W.'

" No general register of deaths was kept at the time of the incident here related, and we have exhausted every means to discover a notice of the death, without success. But we have procured a certificate of Mercy Cox's burial, which took place on January 11, 1829. This is quite compatible with the statement that the death was on January 1st (though such an interval, even in winter, is no doubt unusual), as the lady was buried in a family vault, and probably a lead coffin had to be made. January 1st would be, at the very least, a day of very critical illness. As to the date of the apparition, the marked character of New Year's Day decidedly favours the probability that Miss W.'s memory is correct.

" In answer to inquiries, Miss W. says :

" 'I was born in 1819. The death of my aunt took place in 1829. Though to my most intimate

friends—as Sir Philip Crampton, the late Earl and
Countesses (2) of Dunraven—I have often mentioned the event (and to Judge Halliburton), I
think I never wrote it fully except for Lord Dunraven and his mother, in 1850, who were very
desirous to publish it, but I declined.   I think that
a great reason I have always had for not talking
of it was the awe with which it inspired my mother,
and her strict commands that " I should not mention it to anybody." Then, too, I went to school
and lost sight of Lavinia Cumberland, and I shrank
from the comments of strangers.'

" In conversation Miss W. added that she had
never experienced any other hallucination ; also
that the Cumberland girls had visited her home,
and seen her aunt—which accounts for Lavinia's
recognition of the figure.

" [We learn through a relative of Miss Lavinia
Cumberland that she herself does not recall the
incident ; but that she remembers hearing her
sister speak of a ' ghost case ' in which they had
both been somehow concerned.] "

The following case Mr. Myers contributes to
" Phantasms of the Living " (Vol. II,
p. 305), and he remarks that it is a narrative
of whose accuracy there is no reason to doubt,
as the narrator, Dr. O. B. Ormsby—who wrote
from a place called Murphysborough, Illinois,
U.S.A., in 1884—had been in communication
with Mr. Myers, and replied to his questions.

The narrative, which I abridge, is as follows :

In 1862 Dr. Ormsby was acting as Assistant Surgeon to the 18th Illinois Volunteers ; the regiment having gone forward to attack Fort Henry, he was left behind in charge of the sick.   Among these was a young man called Albert Adams, a sergeant-major, in whom the doctor seems to have been specially interested.   He removed him from the hospital and took him into a private house ; the adjoining apartment to that occupied by the patient was divided from his room only by a thin partition ; this other room was occupied by the doctor's wife.

The man was dying and all the afternoon he could only speak in whispers ; his father was sent for, and at 11 p.m. Sergeant Adams to all appearance died.   Dr. Ormsby, who was at the time standing beside the father by the bed, states that, thinking the bereaved man might faint in the keenness of his grief, he led him away to a chair in the back part of the room, and himself returned to the bedside, intending to close the eyes of Adams, who he thought had expired.   Dr. Ormsby then states : " As I reached the bedside the supposed dead man looked suddenly up in my face, and said, ' Doctor, what day is it ? '   I told him the day of the month, and he answered, ' That is the day I died.'   His father had sprung to the bedside, and Adams turning his eyes on him said, ' Father, our boys have taken Fort Henry, and Charlie (his brother) isn't hurt. I've seen mother and the children, and they are well.'

" He then gave comprehensive directions regarding his funeral, speaking of the corpse as ' my body,' and occupying, I should think, as much as five minutes. He then turned towards me and again said, ' Doctor, what day is it? ' and I answered him as before. He again repeated, ' That's the day I died,' and instantly *was* dead. His tones were quite full and distinct, and so loud as to be readily heard in the adjoining room, and were so heard by Mrs. Ormsby.

" (Signed)   O. B. ORMSBY, M.D."

In reply to further questions, Dr. Ormsby wrote that he had no opportunity to learn whether what was said about the mother and children was correct, but that he learned afterwards that Fort Henry was taken, and the brother was uninjured.

CHAPTER V

MUSIC HEARD AT THE TIME OF DEATH BY THE DYING OR BY PERSONS PRESENT AT A DEATH-BED

AMONG the numerous cases in which music is heard at the time of death, the following incident, well attested by different observers, is quoted from " Phantasms of the Living," Vol. II, p. 639 :

A master of Eton College, Mr. L., wrote to Mr. Gurney in February, 1884, enclosing a memorandum which was made shortly after the death of his mother, which occurred in 1881.

It appears that at the time of her death there were several persons present in the room, namely, the Matron of Mr. L.'s house (Miss H.), a middle-aged, experienced woman ; the doctor in attendance (Dr. G.) ; a friend of the dying lady (Miss I.) ; and two other persons (Eliza W. and Charlotte C.).

Immediately after Mrs. L.'s death, Miss H. and Charlotte C. left the room to procure something, and shortly after they had left Miss I. heard a sound of " low, soft music, exceedingly sweet, as of three girls' voices." It seemed to come from the street and passed away. Dr. G. also heard it and went to the window to look out. No one could be seen outside in the street. Eliza W. who was in the room also heard a sound as of " very low, sweet singing." Mr. L. himself, who sends the memorandum, heard nothing. The two others who had left the room, Miss H. and Charlotte C., distinctly heard the sound of singing as they were coming upstairs.

Later on, when those present were talking over the matter, they found that each one of them had heard the sound of singing and music—*except Mr. L.*

It was specially noticeable that the staircase, up which Miss H. and Charlotte C. were coming, was at the back of the house and away from the street. The time of Mrs. L.'s death was about 2 a.m. on July 28, 1881.

In reply to inquiries Miss I. sent the following memorandum which she made *immediately after* the death of her friend, Mrs. L. ; it is as follows :

" *July* 28*th*, 1881

" Just after dear Mrs. L.'s death between 2 and 3 a.m., I heard a most sweet and singular strain of singing outside the windows ; it died away after passing the house. All in the room [except Mr. L.] heard it, and the medical attendant, who was still with us, went to the window, as I did, and looked

out, but there was nobody. It was a bright and
beautiful night. It was as if several voices were
singing in perfect unison a most sweet melody
which died away in the distance. Two persons
had gone from the room to fetch something and
were coming upstairs *at the back of the house* and
heard the singing and stopped, saying, ' What is
that singing ? ' They could not, *naturally*, have
heard any sound from outside the windows in the
front of the house from where they were at the
back.

" E. I."

Dr. G., who was in attendance upon Mrs. L.,
writes to Mr. Gurney in 1884, as follows :

" Eton, Windsor
" I remember the circumstance perfectly. I was
sent for about midnight, and remained with Mrs. L.
until her death about 2.30 a.m. Shortly after we
heard a few bars of lovely music, not unlike that
from an æolian harp—and it filled the air for a few
seconds. I went to the window and looked out,
thinking there must be someone outside, but could
see no one though it was quite light and clear.
Strangely enough, those outside the room heard the
same sounds, as they were coming upstairs quite at
the other side of the door [house]."

Mr. Gurney adds a note that as Mr. L.,
although present at the time of his mother's
death, did *not* share the experience of the

others, this is strong evidence that the sounds did not come from any persons singing outside the house, and the other evidence quoted confirms this.

There are, however, many cases in which the dying persons or those near the bedside have heard musical sounds which could not be attributed to any earthly source. These sounds may have their origin, in some cases at least, in the minds of the living.

The following case appears to point to a hallucinatory origin of the music heard. It is an interesting case and worth quoting in an abbreviated form. It is printed in the " S.P.R. Journal," Vol. IV, p. 181.

Here the subject was a deaf mute, John Britton, who was taken dangerously ill with rheumatic fever, which caused his hands and fingers—which were his only means of conversation—to become so swollen that he could not use them, greatly to the distress of his relatives, to whom he could not make known his wants nor his sufferings.

The narrator, Mr. S. Allen, Steward of Haileybury College, and a brother-in-law of John Britton, states that the doctor thinking John could not recover, they had sent for members of his family. He adds that when he and his wife were in a room below John's bedroom, they were greatly surprised to hear music coming from upstairs, and ran up at once to find out what it was. He narrates as follows :

" We found Jack lying on his back with his eyes fixed on the ceiling, and his face lighted up with the brightest of smiles. After a little while Jack awoke and used the words ' Heaven ' and ' beautiful ' as well as he could by means of his lips and facial expression. As he became more conscious he also told us in the same manner that his brother Tom and his sister Harriet were coming to see him. This we considered very unlikely as they lived some distance off, but shortly afterwards a cab drove up from which they alighted. They had sent no intimation of their coming, nor had anyone else. After Jack's partial recovery, when he was able to write or converse upon his fingers, he told us that he had been allowed to see into Heaven and to hear most beautiful music."

Mr. Allen asks, " How did John know that Tom and Harriet were travelling, and how could he have heard these musical sounds which we also heard ? " He remarks that the music could not have come from next door or from the street, and he gives a rough plan of his house to show that it was not in a row, and that the sounds could not be due to any normal cause.

Mrs. Allen confirms her husband's statement, and says that she heard the sounds of singing which came from her brother's bedroom, and that when she entered the bedroom he was in a comatose state and smiling, and his lips were moving as if he were in conversation with someone, but no sound came from them. Mrs. Allen continues, " when he had recovered sufficiently to use his hands he told me more details of what he had seen, and used the words ' beautiful music.' " She adds that her brother died a few years later, and states " the nurse and I were watching in the room, my brother was looking just as he did on the former occasion, smiling, and he said quite distinctly and articulately ' Angels ' and ' Home.' "

The Rev. L. S. Milford, a master at Haileybury College, in giving an account of the interview he had with Mr. and Mrs. Allen, states that " Mrs. Allen says the sounds she heard resembled singing—sweet music without distinguishable words—that she went upstairs directly she heard the music, which continued until she reached the bedroom. Mr. Allen's impression is that the sound resembled the full notes of an organ or of an aeolian harp."

The following interesting case is an instance in which the dying person heard the sound of

singing and also had a vision of a lady of whose
death she was unaware. The case is taken
from the " Proceedings S.P.R." for 1885,[1]
and is as follows somewhat abridged :

Mrs. Z., wife of Col. Z. (a well-known Irish gentleman who does not wish his name published), was
having some friends to stay with her and asked a
Miss X., who was training as a professional singer,
to spend a week with her and help to entertain her
guests. This she did. Several years later Mrs. Z.
became very ill and expected to die ; she was,
however, perfectly composed and in the full possession of her senses, and was anxious to arrange some
business affairs. For this purpose her husband
came to her bedside and talked over these matters
with her. Suddenly she changed the subject and
said to her husband, " Do you hear those voices
singing ? " Col. Z., who narrates the incident,
replied that he did not, and his wife continued, " I
have heard them several times to-day, and I am
sure they are the angels welcoming me to Heaven,
but," she added, " it is strange, there is one voice
among them I am sure I know, but I cannot
remember whose voice it is." Suddenly she
stopped and said, pointing straight over her husband's head, " Why, there she is in the corner of
the room ; it is Julia X. She is coming on ; she
is leaning over you ; she has her hands up ; she is
praying. Do look ; she is going." Her husband

[1] See " Proceedings S.P.R.," Vol. III, pp. 92, 93 ; also
" Human Personality," Vol. II, p. 339.

turned round but could see nothing. His wife then said, " She has gone."

These things the Colonel at the time believed to be merely the phantasms of a dying person, but two days afterwards on taking up " The Times " newspaper, he saw recorded in it the death of Julia, who some years previously had married a Mr. Webley. He was so astounded that a day or two after his wife's funeral he went to see Julia's father, and asked if his daughter were really dead. " Yes," he said, " poor thing, she died of puerperal fever, and on the day she died she began singing, and sang on and on till she died."

In a subsequent communication from Colonel Z. the following facts were given :

Mrs. Webley (*née* Julia X.) died on February 2, 1874.

Mrs. Z. (wife of Colonel Z.) died on February 13, 1874.

Colonel Z. saw notice of Mrs. Webley's death on February 14, 1874.

Mrs. Z. never was subject to hallucinations of any sort.

Mr. Gurney subsequently received a note from Mr. Webley (husband of Julia) in which he stated that beautiful as his wife's voice was, it never had been so exquisitely beautiful as when she sang just before her death.

John Bunyan relates an incident of this kind which is worth quoting, though its evidential value is not very great.

He states :

" Talking of the dying of Christians, I will tell you a story of one that died some time since in our town. The man was a godly old Puritan, for so the godly were called in times past. This man, after a long and godly life, fell sick, of the sickness whereof he died. And as he lay drawing on, the woman that looked to him thought she heard music, and that the sweetest that ever she heard in her life, which also continued until he gave up the ghost. Now, when his soul departed from him the music seemed to withdraw, and to go further and further off from the house, and so it went until the sound was quite gone out of hearing." [1]

[1] See Bunyan's " Works." Edited by George Offor, Vol. III, pp. 653, 654. Glasgow, 1855.

CHAPTER VI

VISIONS OF THE SPIRIT OF A DYING PERSON LEAVING THE BODY

THE following case, which is taken from the " S.P.R. Journal" (Vol. XIII, pp. 308–311), was sent to Dr. Hodgson by Dr. Burgess, an Associate of the American S.P.R. The vision was seen only by the husband of the dying woman, and by none of the others present in the room. The doctor who was present, Dr. Renz, testifies that the percipient, Mr. G., " was in a perfectly normal state before and after, and that there were features in the vision that would not have been likely to occur to him."

The percipient, Mr. G., states as follows :

" My wife died at 11.45 p.m. on Friday, May 23rd, 1902. Gathered round the bedside were some of our most intimate friends, the physician in attendance, and two trained nurses. I was seated at the bedside holding my wife's hand. . . . Earlier in the evening, at 6.45, I happened to look towards the door, when I saw floating through the doorway three separate and distinct clouds in strata. Each cloud appeared to be about four feet in length, from six to eight inches in width, the lower one about two feet from the ground, the others at intervals of about six inches. . . . Slowly

these clouds approached the bed until they completely enveloped it.   Then, gazing through the
mist, I beheld standing at the head of my dying
wife a woman's figure about three feet in height,
transparent, yet like a sheen of brightest gold ; a
figure so glorious in its appearance that no words
can be used fitly to describe it.   She was dressed
in the Grecian costume, with long, loose and flowing
sleeves—upon her head a brilliant crown.   In all
its splendour and beauty the figure remained
motionless with hands uplifted over my wife,
seeming to express a welcome with a quiet, glad
countenance, with a dignity of calmness and peace.
Two figures in white knelt by my wife's side,
apparently leaning towards her ; other figures
hovered about the bed, more or less distinct.

" Above my wife, and connected with a cord
proceeding from her forehead, over the left eye,
there floated in a horizontal position a nude, white
figure, apparently her ' astral body.'   At times the
suspended figure would lie perfectly quiet, at other
times it would shrink in size until it was no larger
than perhaps eighteen inches, but always the figure
was perfect and distinct. . . .

" This vision, or whatever it may be called, I
saw continuously during the five hours preceding
the death of my wife.   All through those five hours
I felt a strange feeling of oppression and weight
upon my head and limbs. . . .

" At last the fatal moment arrived ; with a gasp,
the astral figure struggling, my wife ceased to
breathe ; she apparently was dead : however, a

few seconds later she breathed again, twice, and then all was still. With her last breath and last gasp, as the soul left the body, the cord was severed suddenly and the astral figure vanished. The clouds and the spirit forms disappeared instantly, and, strange to say, all the oppression that weighed upon me was gone ; I was myself, cool, calm, and deliberate, able to direct, from the moment of death, the disposition of the body, its preparation for a final resting-place.

" I leave my readers to determine whether I was labouring under a mental delusion caused by anxiety, sorrow and fatigue, or if a glimpse of a spirit world of beauty, happiness, calmness, and peace was granted to my mortal eyes."

The doctor who was present writes as follows :

" From my own observations I can most positively put aside a temporary acute state of hallucinatory insanity during the time of the vision just recorded. . . . I knew Mr. G. well, and I had occasion to know that he never read anything in the occult line ; that everything that was not a proven fact was incompatible with his positive mind—so much so that during his vision (of which I did not know at the time) he asked me frequently if I thought he was going to become insane. . . .

" As soon as Mrs. G. was dead, Mr. G., who for six hours was sitting almost motionless next to her, rose and gave all his orders in such a calm and business-like way that it surprised all who were present. If he had laboured under a hallucination his mind would not have become clear as suddenly as it did. It is now 2½ weeks since the death and the vision. Mr. G. is absolutely normal physically as well as mentally. He has attended to his business as usual, and, besides, fulfilled many extraordinary duties.

" (Signed) C. RENZ "

Many well authenticated cases are on record where the relatives of a person, watching by the death-bed, have seen at the moment of death a cloudy form rising from the body of the deceased and hovering for a time in the room and then passing away.

Lady Mount Temple informed me that something of this kind was noticed by a psychic friend of hers, who was present at the death of Lord Mount Temple. Others present did not see it.

In a letter that has recently been sent me of a late well-known dignitary of the Church (a Dean) in New South Wales, he describes the death of his son a few years ago.

He says that at about 3.30 p.m. he and his wife were standing one on each side of the bed and bending over their dying son, when just as his breathing ceased they both saw " something rise as it were from his face like a delicate veil or mist, and slowly pass away." He adds, " We were deeply impressed and remarked, ' How wonderful! Surely that must be the departure of his spirit.' We were not at all distracted so as to be mistaken in what we saw."

The following cases are recorded by Mrs. Joy Snell, in her book, " The Ministry of Angels " :

" It was about six months after I began work in the hospital that it was revealed to me that the dying often really do see those who have come from the realms of spirit life to welcome them on their entrance into another state of existence.

" The first time that I received this ocular proof was at the death of Laura Stirman, a sweet girl of seventeen, who was a personal friend of mine. She was a victim of consumption. She suffered no pain, but the weariness that comes from extreme weakness and debility was heavy upon her and she yearned for rest.

" A short time before she expired I became aware that two spirit forms were standing by the bedside, one on either side of it. I did not see them enter the room ; they were standing by the bedside when they first became visible to me, but I could see them as distinctly as I could any of the human occupants of the room. I recognized their faces as those of two girls who had been the closest friends of the girl who was dying. They had passed away a year before and were then about her own age.

" Just before they appeared the dying girl exclaimed, ' It has grown suddenly dark ; I cannot see anything ! ' But she recognized them immediately. A smile, beautiful to see, lit up her face. She stretched forth her hands and in joyous tones exclaimed, ' Oh, you have come to take me away ! I am glad, for I am very tired.'

" As she stretched forth her hands the two angels extended each a hand, one grasping the dying girl's right hand, the other her left hand. Their faces were illumined by a smile more radiantly beautiful even than that of the face of the girl who was so soon to find the rest for which she longed. She did not speak again, but for nearly a minute her hands remained outstretched, grasped by the hands of the angels, and she continued to gaze at them with the glad light in her eyes and the smile on her face.

" Her father, mother, and brother, who had been summoned that they might be present when the end came, began to weep bitterly, for they knew that she was leaving them. From my heart there went up a prayer that they might see what I saw, but they could not.

" The angels seemed to relax their grasp of the girl's hands, which then fell back on the bed. A sigh came from her lips, such as one might give who resigns himself gladly to a much-needed sleep, and in another moment she was what the world calls dead. But that sweet smile with which she had first recognized the angels was still stamped on her features.

" The two angels remained by the bedside during the brief space that elapsed before the spirit form took shape above the body in which physical life had ceased. Then they rose and stood for a few moments one on each side of her, who was now like unto themselves ; and three angels went from the room where a short time before there had been only two."

" About a month after the death of Laura Stirman, which I have just related, another friend of mine died in the hospital, a Mr. Campbell, a man of 45. It was pneumonia that carried him off. He was a good and devout man and for him death held no terrors, for he was sure that it was but the transition to a happier, more exalted life than can be lived here. His only regret at dying was that he would leave behind him a dearly-loved wife ; but that regret was softened by the assurance that their parting would be only for a time, and that she would join him some day in that other world whither he was going.

" She was sitting by his bed, and, believing as he believed, was awaiting the end with resignation. About an hour before he died he called her by name, and pointing upwards, said, ' Look, L——, there is B—— ! He is waiting for me. And now he smiles and holds out his hands to me. Can't you see him ? ' ' No, dear, I cannot see him,' she replied, ' but I know that he is there because you see him.' B—— was their only child who had been taken from them about a year before, when between five and six years of age. I could plainly see the little angel with curly flaxen hair and blue eyes, and garbed in what I call the spirit robe. The face was just that of a winsome child, but etherealized and radiant as no earthly faces ever are.

" The father had been greatly weakened by the ravages of his disease, and the joyful emotion occasioned by seeing his angel child seemed to exhaust what little vitality he had left. He closed his eyes and sank into a placid sleep. He remained in that state for about an hour, the angel child meanwhile staying poised above the bed with an expression of glad expectancy on his radiant face. Occasionally he looked lovingly at his mother.

" The breathing of the dying man grew fainter and fainter until it ceased altogether. Then again I witnessed what had now become a familiar spectacle to me—the formation of the spirit body above the discarded earthly body. When it was complete the angel child grasped the hand of the now angel father, each gazed into the eyes of the other with an expression of the tenderest affection, and with faces aglow with joy and happiness they vanished.

" Later on in the day, the widow (Mrs. Campbell) said to me ' I am very glad my dear husband saw B—— before he died ; it was natural that B—— should come for him to take him to the angels, for they loved each other dearly. I shall now be able to think of them as always together and happy.

And when I receive my summons I know that they will both come for me.'

" After I had left the hospital and had taken up private nursing I was engaged to nurse an old lady (Mrs. Barton, aged 60), who was suffering from a painful internal disease. She was a widow and her only daughter lived with her. . . . The time came when the end was very near. The mother had been for some time unconscious, and the daughter was kneeling by the bedside, weeping, her face buried in her hands. Suddenly two angels became visible to me, standing on either side of the bed. The face of one was that of a man who, when he departed from this life, was apparently about 60 years of age. His beard and hair were iron-grey ; but there was stamped on his features that indescribable something indicative of exuberant vitality and vigour, which shines forth from all angel faces I have seen, whether in other respects they present the semblance of youth or old age. The face of the other angel was that of a woman, apparently some ten or fifteen years younger.

" The dying woman opened her eyes, and into them there came that look of glad recognition I have so often observed in those whose spirits are about to be released for ever from their earthly tenements. She stretched forth her two hands. One angel grasped one hand and the other angel the other hand, while their radiant faces were aglow with the joy of welcoming to the better world her whose earthly pilgrimage was finished.

" ' Oh, Willie,' she exclaimed, ' you have come to take me home at last, and I am glad, for my sufferings have been hard to bear and I am very tired.' Then she added, ' And you too, Martha ! ' With the joyous light still in her eyes her hands remained outstretched for perhaps half a minute. Then they seemed to slip from the grasp of the angels. All her sufferings were over.

" The daughter had raised her head at the sound of her mother's voice, and her tear-dimmed eyes seemed to reflect something of the glad surprise depicted on her mother's face.

" ' I can doubt no more after this,' she said to me when her mother had breathed her last breath ; ' I know that mother saw father and her sister, Aunt Martha. I know that they came to take her to her rest in heaven.'

" Eagerly she listened to me when I told her a little later how I had seen two angels depart with her angel mother. ' I believe it ! I believe it ! ' she cried, ' but, oh, how I wish that I could have seen it too ! ' "

SELECTED PAPERS BY SIR WILLIAM BARRETT FROM THE PROCEEDINGS OF THE SOCIETY FOR PSYCHICAL RESEARCH

ON SOME PHENOMENA ASSOCIATED WITH ABNORMAL CONDITIONS OF MIND.*

There are certain conditions of the mind, either temporarily. induced or habitual, which appear to be associated with many remarkable phenomena that have hitherto received but partial attention from scientific men. On various occasions during the last ten years I have had the opportunity of observing some of these singular states, and in the hope of eliciting further information or of stimulating inquiry by those more competent than myself, I venture to bring the following facts under the notice of the British Association.

The observations to be described belong mainly to the class known by the names of mesmerism, hypnotism, or induced somnambulism, for these terms express very similar mental stages. The experiments of the late Dr. Braid have led physiologists to recognise the existence of the fact that an extraordinary condition of the mind can be induced in certain susceptible or sensitive individuals by merely fixing the attention rigidly for several minutes upon any bright object. Whilst staying with a friend in Westmeath, now some years ago, I had the opportunity of frequently witnessing the production of this morbid condition, and, further, of observing some phenomena that are usually denied by eminent physiologists of the present day.

Selecting some of the village children and placing them in a quiet room, giving each some small object to look at steadily, it was found that one amongst the number readily passed into a state of reverie, resembling that dreamy condition between sleeping and waking. In this state the subject could readily be made to believe the most extravagant statements, such as that the table was a mountain, a chair a pony, a mark on the floor an insuperable obstacle. As Dr. Maudsley observes in his *Mental Physiology*, "the mind of the patient becomes possessed with the ideas the operator suggests, so that his body becomes an automatic machine set in motion by them."

In the Proceedings of the British Association for 1855, is a paper by Mr. Braid in which the phenomena of mesmerism are referred to

---

* This paper was originally read before the British Association, at the Glasgow Meeting, September, 1876. By permission of the Council of the S.P.R., it was included in the proceedings of the meeting on April 24th, after a verbal revision and the omission of a few paragraphs. Though this paper was the subject of much animadversion when first read, students of the Reports published by the S.P.R. will be able to judge how far the opinions expressed seven years ago have since received confirmation.

what is termed a mono-ideo-dynamic action, the ideo-motor force of the present day. Many other writers might be quoted, but the main facts are not now denied ; in fact, this peculiar physiological state is referred to in all recent works on the mind.

The fact that one mind can thus readily be thrown into a state of passive obedience to another mind is undoubtedly a fact of much importance. It is important, not only as exhibiting a state into which certain minds are liable to be exposed, but also as probably affording a clue to some of the extraordinary assertions that have been made by credible witnesses as to the elongation and levitation of the human body, the handling of fire and the like. . These facts are testified to by eminent men whose word one cannot for a moment question. Either the narrators *saw* the things they describe or they *thought* they saw them. The following considerations seem to render it highly probable that the latter affords a provisional explanation.

Mr. Herbert Spencer has compared the ordinarily vivid mental impressions produced by the perceptions of external things which are simultaneously present in our consciousness with the fainter ideas produced by reflection, memory, or imagination—to two parallel streams of consciousness, constantly varying in their relative breadth, as the outer or the inner world predominates. During states of activity we are receiving a crowd of impressions from the senses, and hence the stream of consciousness derived from the external world causes the faint manifestations derived from within to sink into insignificance. But when the vivid manifestations produced by the senses are enfeebled—*e.g.*, by closing the eyes, stillness, &c.—the usually faint stream of consciousness becomes predominant ; the heterogeneous current of ideas grows more distinct, and almost excludes the vivid order of impressions, and finally, on lapsing into sleep, the manifestations of the vivid order cease to be distinguishable as such, and those of the faint order come to be mistaken for them.

It is highly probable that the vivid stream of consciousness produced by sensation, having been reduced by quietness and twilight, the minds of those who testify to the feats referred to, would readily yield themselves to any emphatic suggestion on the part of the operator. However, to put this matter to the test of experiment, I selected (in the manner already described) a young lad, who in the course of fifteen minutes was hypnotised, as Mr. Braid would say. The lad now readily believed any assertion I made, with evident relish going through the farce of eating and drinking because I suggested the act, though the only materials I gave him were a book and an empty vase. When subsequently he partly awoke, he was under the conviction that he had had his tea, yet could not understand how it was, as he associated the actual books with the forced idea of bread and butter, and the struggle of reason and memory, was curious to witness. On another occasion, when the lad was hypnotised, I placed my shoes on the table and forcibly drew his attention to them. I then suggested that I was standing in them, and after he had given his assent, I said, "Now I am going to rise up and float round the room." So saying I raised my hand, and directing his sight upwards, pointed out the successive stages in my imaginary flight, and on my slowly depressing my hand, and asserting I was once more on the ground, he drew a sigh of relief. On awakening he held to the belief that I had in some indistinct way floated round the room and pointed to the course I had taken. I had not the slightest doubt that after a few trials, this extravagant idea might have been fixed in the lad's mind with the greatest ease.

I adduce the foregoing experiment to shew the powerful influence of *suggestion* when the mind is in certain states such as rêverie, and hence the need of guarding against illusion. At the same time, I do not wish it to be supposed that I dogmatically assert this must have been the explanation of the phenomena described by Lord Lindsay and others ; all I assert is, in our present state of knowledge, it is an easier explanation than to assume the actual occurrence of the marvels. Nevertheless, in justice to those who hold an opposite view, I am bound to mention a case that came under my own repeated observation, wherein certain inexplicable physical phenomena occurred in broad daylight, and for which I could find no satisfactory solution either on the ground of hallucination or of fraud.*   . . .

Returning to the experience gained at my friend's house in Westmeath, the girl there mesmerised passed on another occasion into a state of deeper sleep or trance, wherein no sensation whatever was experienced unless accompanied by pressure over the eyebrows of the subject. When the pressure of the fingers was removed, the girl fell back in her chair utterly unconscious of all around, and had lost all control over her voluntary muscles. On re-applying the pressure, though her eyes remained closed, she sat up and answered questions readily, but the manner in which she answered them, her acts and expressions, were capable of wonderful diversity by merely altering the place on the head where the pressure was applied. So sudden and marked were the changes produced by a movement of the fingers that the operation seemed very like playing on some musical instrument.† I mention these facts simply to ask whether a careful and systematic study of them

---

* The description of this case is here omitted, not from any doubt of its genuineness, but because it is thought better to refer it to the special Committee of the Society appointed to deal with this class of phenomena.

† The deep mesmeric sleep and the complete insensibility of the subject seemed to be the best guarantee against a clever course of deception on her part.

might not throw some additional light on the localisation of the functions of the brain. For extraordinary as it may appear that moderate pressure on the skull could produce any local irritation of the brain, yet it must be borne in mind that we are here dealing with the brain in an abnormal condition, probably a state of unstable equilibrium, so that a slight disturbance might produce an altogether disproportionate effect.

On a third occasion the subject, after passing through what has been termed the "biological" and "phrenological" states, became at length keenly and wonderfully sensitive to the voice or acts of the operator. It was impossible for the latter to call the girl by her name, however faintly and inaudibly to those around, without at once eliciting a prompt response. Even when the operator left the house, and at intervals gently called the girl's name, at the same time indicating the fact by signs to those within sight, she still responded, more and more faintly, it is true, as the distance became greater. This extraordinary and unnatural sensibility surprised me greatly, as it exceeded anything I had heard or read, and I regretted being unable, at the time, to carry out more experiments in this direction.

In his *Mental Physiology*, Dr. Carpenter states that he has seen abundant evidence that the sensibility of a hypnotised subject may be exalted to an extraordinary degree in regard to some particular class of impressions, this being due to the concentration of the whole attention upon the objects which excited them. Thus, he has known a youth in the hypnotised state find out, by the sense of smell, the owner of a glove which was placed in his hand, from amongst a party of more than sixty persons, scenting at each of them one after the other, until he came to the right individual. In another case, the owner of a ring was unhesitatingly found out from amongst a company of twelve, the ring having been withdrawn from the finger before the somnambule was introduced. He has seen other cases, again, in which the sense of temperature was extraordinarily exalted, very slight differences, inappreciable to ordinary touch, being at once detected.

Without denying the possibility of such an extraordinary sensibility, other facts I witnessed pointed in the direction of a *community of sensation* between the mesmeriser and the subject, for I noticed that if the operator tasted, smelt, or touched anything, or experienced any sudden sensation of warmth or cold, a corresponding effect was instantly produced on the subject, though nothing was said, nor could the subject have seen what had taken place upon the operator. To be assured of this, I bandaged the girl's eyes with great care, and the operator having gone behind the girl to the other end of the room, I watched him and the girl, and repeatedly assured myself of this fact. If he placed his hand over the lighted lamp, the girl instantly withdrew hers, as if in pain; if he tasted salt or sugar, corresponding expressions of dislike and approval were indicated by the girl. If, however, anyone else in the room other than the operator tried the experiment, I could perceive no indications on the part of the subject. Certainly, so far as my observations extended, there did seem to be a vast difference between the influence exerted on the subject by the operator, and that which could be exerted by anyone else. Dr. Carpenter believes, however, that there is no foundation for the "*rapport*" which is so often asserted to exist between a mesmerised subject and the operator. On this point he remarks : " If the subject be ' possessed ' with the previous conviction that a particular individual is destined to exert a special influence over him, the suggestions of that individual are obviously received with greater readiness, and are responded to with greater certainty, than are those of any bystander. This is the whole mystery of the relationship between the ' biologiser ' and his ' subject.' "

For my own part, I do not think that the whole mystery of this so-called "*rapport*" can be disposed of quite so easily. Not only do the facts I have just given negative Dr. Carpenter's easy solution, but the following still more remarkable experiments shew, at any rate, that the question is one deserving of more extended inquiry.

When the subject was in the state of trance or profound hypnotism, I noticed that not only sensations but also ideas or emotions occurring in the operator appeared to be reproduced in the subject without the intervention of any sign, or visible or audible communication. Having mesmerised the girl myself, I took a card at random from a pack that was in a drawer in another room. Glancing at the card to see what it was, I placed it within a book, and in this state brought it to the girl. Giving her the closed book, I asked her to tell me what I had put within its leaves. She held the book close to the side of her head and said, " I see something inside with red spots on it." " Count the spots," I told her ; she did so, and said there were five red spots. The card was the five of diamonds. Another card, chosen and concealed in a similar way, was also correctly named ; and when a Bank of Ireland note was substituted she said, " Oh now I see a number of heads ; so many I can't count them." She sometimes failed to guess correctly, asserting the things were dim, and invariably I found she could give me no information of what was within the book, unless I had previously known what it was myself. More remarkable still, I asked her to go in imagination to Regent Street, in London, and tell me what shops she saw. The girl had never been out of her remote Irish village, but she correctly described to me the shop of Mr. Ladd, the optician, of which I happened to be thinking— referring to some large crystals (of Iceland spar) and to other things in the shop—and when she mentally left the shop she noticed the large clock that overhangs the entrance to Beak Street.

In many other ways I convinced myself that the existence of a distinct idea in my own mind gave rise to an image of the idea in the subject's mind; not always a clear image, but one that could not fail to be recognised as a more or less distorted reflection of my own thought. The important point is that every care was taken to prevent any unconscious movement of the lips, or otherwise giving any indication to the subject, although one could hardly reveal the contents of an optician's shop by facial indications.*

This power of "thought-reading," as it has been termed, has often been described by writers on mesmerism, but little credence has been given to it by physiologists or psychologists.

Some assert that this state extends even further; that subjects in this condition are able to perceive occurrences at remote distances which are not known to any present, and yet are subsequently verified. I

* The following interesting communication from my friend, Mr. W. E. Wilson, of Co. Westmeath, reached me in September, 1876, after the foregoing was written, and gives us a glimpse of something even beyond thought-reading, but many more experiments are necessary before a *prima facie* case in favour of so-called "clairvoyance" can be said to have been established.

Mr. Wilson writes in reference to the above-mentioned card experiment :—

"You are correct, as I remember several experiments of the same kind, I think we proved beyond all doubt that the subject is able to read the thoughts of the mesmeriser. Also that they are able to see through things which are to us optically opaque, provided that they could touch the objects or hold them in their hand. At any distance beyond that I don't think we have evidence that they can see things unless the mesmeriser knows them, in which case it of course becomes thought-reading. A lady subject has often told us the time by a gold hunting watch, which was put in a box after the hands were altered to any extent by the keyless arrangement, so that no one knew their position. I remember one instance with her. There were some friends in the room looking on. The hands of the watch were twisted round promiscuously; it was then put in a box and the closed box put in her hand. She at once said what o'clock it was. My father opened the watch to see if she was right, but found to his astonishment that she was wrong. He told her so, and gave her the watch to try again. She at once said she was right. He told her to look again, but she got crusty and refused to look for some time. He pressed her to look once more. She still said she was right, but that it was now a minute past the time she first said. My father opened the watch to shew those present the mistake she made, but found that she was perfectly right, that he had made a mistake himself. In that instance the thoughts of the mesmeriser were against her. Another instance I remember was with a country boy. He was mesmerised in a room which we made perfectly dark. Cards were given to him at random from a pack. He told fourteen correctly without a mistake, and I have no doubt would have gone through the pack if we liked. Of course you know that they don't try to use the eyes to see with. They always, without exception, put whatever is put in their hand to the side of their head, a little behind the ear, and about six inches from them. They always say that everything is greatly diminished. Ordinary book print they describe as fine lines."

have had cases of this kind described to me by those whom I esteem as careful and conscientious observers ; but as nothing of the sort has ever come under my own observation, I refrain from stating what I cannot vouch for myself. Even as regards the facts 1 have myself witnessed, I do not pretend that they do more than justify further inquiry, as a large amount of similar evidence must be obtained by well qualified men before these phenomena can be accepted unreservedly. All I wish to urge is, that it is not wise to allow a natural feeling of incredulity on this matter to become a barrier to a possible extension of knowledge.

Dr. Carpenter himself remarks, that " everyone who admits that ' there are more things in heaven and earth than are dreamt of in our philosophy,' will be wise in maintaining ' a reserve of possibility ' as to phenomena which are not altogether opposed to the laws of physics or physiology, but rather transcend them "; and he adds *(Mental Physiology,* p. 633), " some of his own experiences have led him to suspect that a power of intuitively perceiving what is passing in the mind of another, which has been designated as ' thought-reading,' may, like certain forms of sense-perception, be extraordinarily exalted by entire concentration of the attention. So far, however, as we are acquainted with the conditions of its exercise, it seems to depend upon the unconscious interpretation of indications (many of them indefinable) furnished by the expression of the countenance, by style of conversation, and by various involuntary movements ; that interpretation, however, going, in many instances, far beyond what can have been learned by experience as the *meaning* of such indications."

It will be noticed that whilst Dr. Carpenter does not deny the possibility of thought-reading or some analogous kind of divining power, he distinctly asserts that everything *he* has seen is explicable by sign or "muscle-reading." The evidence that I have here adduced, on the other hand, indicates that when a person is thrown into a hypnotic or passive condition, the nervous action associated with thought can be excited by a corresponding action in an adjoining individual, and this across space and *without* the intervention of the recognised organs of sensation. Nor does this seem an altogether incredible fact. The energy of electricity exerts itself in two ways, by transmission along a material conductor and by influence, or induction as it is termed, across space. May not nerve energy, whatever be its nature, also act by influence as well as conduction ? For many years I have held this view, and it has been confirmed by what I have witnessed from time to time. My main object in bringing this paper before the Section is to direct attention to the subject in the hope that those who have any evidence to offer in support of this view, or any good grounds for opposing it, may favour me with their experience.

PROCEEDINGS

OF THE

Society for Psychical Research

PART XLVIII.

MARCH, 1904.

ADDRESS BY THE PRESIDENT.

PROFESSOR W. F. BARRETT, F.R.S.

January 29th, 1904.

MY first duty is to thank you most heartily for the honour
you have conferred upon me to-day. When I recall the names
of the illustrious men who have preceded me in this chair, I
can only ask your indulgence for the deficiencies of which I am
very conscious and express the hope that our Society may not
suffer from having chosen as its President one from a remote
distance, and who can lay no claim to the eminence of his
predecessors.

It has not been the custom formally to move a vote of
thanks to our out-going President, but I am sure you would
desire me to voice the grateful appreciation, which we all
sincerely feel, of the great services which Sir Oliver Lodge has
rendered to the Society during his three years' tenure of office.
In his presence I cannot express all I would like to say, but
this much perhaps he will permit, that during his Presidency,
his influence and high position in the ranks of science have
been of inestimable value to the Society, whilst his simple and
unaffected courage has been a noble stimulus to us all.

Here too, perhaps, you will allow me to say how much we owe to the ungrudging and arduous labour of our Hon. Sec. Mr. Piddington, and to the skill and care with which our Hon. Treasurer Mr. H. A. Smith has, almost from the foundation of the Society, conducted its finances, and to the legal advice and assistance, in the incorporation of the Society and other matters, which Mr. Smith and Mr. S. C. Scott have freely given to us. Though I am quite sure they would deprecate any allusion to their services, yet I know you will join with me in expressing our most grateful and cordial thanks to each and all of these gentlemen.

This month we enter upon the 23rd year of our existence, and in spite of the irreparable losses we have suffered in the past through the removal from this life of those who seemed to be the very pillars on which the Society rested,—Gurney, Sidgwick, Myers,—losses which naturally gave rise to many gloomy forebodings—nevertheless we have no reason for despondency, on the contrary the present flourishing condition of our Society far exceeds that which even I, the most sanguine of its founders, could have anticipated. Both numerically and financially we are stronger than we have at any time been; the number of our Members and Associates throughout the United Kingdom, after eliminating all losses through death, etc., is 832; in addition we have 530 Members and Associates in the American Branch, and on the Continent kindred societies are springing up.

As you will see by the printed statement of accounts, our financial condition is also satisfactory, and we have in addition, thanks to a generous legacy, a considerable reserve fund, which we hope the liberality of our members will increase. The Council have placed this reserve fund in the hands of Trustees and have determined to appropriate the interest of it, when it reaches the sum of £8000, to the purpose of experimental research in such subjects as fall within the scope of our Society.

It is true that no original research of any value can ever be made to order. The progress of knowledge in psychical science, as elsewhere, must in the end rest upon the self-sacrificing and intelligent work of those in whom a keen interest for a particular branch of enquiry has been excited, and whose enthusiasm is not stimulated by, nor can it be repaid in, coin of the realm. But the investigator has to live, and to enable him to do so whilst he is conducting any hopeful enquiry, sanctioned by the Council, a modest sum will be appropriated to him as a grant in aid.

We hope to receive from time to time applications from competent enquirers of either sex who will undertake special lines of investigation. It might also be desirable, though here I speak my own opinion only, to follow the examples of the older scientific societies and award medals or premiums for any good piece of original work. There is an immense field for investigation; psychical research is almost virgin ground as far as strict scientific enquiry is concerned, and though the worker is not likely in this generation to meet with much encouragement from the world at large, and still less any benefit to himself, he may be sure his toil will not be in vain. I would therefore earnestly appeal to any members or friends of our Society to give us what help they can; if personal assistance is not possible, their contributions to the completion of our research fund will be gratefully welcomed.[1]

And this brings me to a point to which for a moment it is desirable to refer. The work of the Society has hitherto been in comparatively few hands, and the centre of gravity of the Society inevitably falls in that place (such as Cambridge) where the most active workers are or have been found. This has led some of our members to feel perhaps a little aggrieved that the centre is not within their own precincts, that they are not more in touch with the work of the Society, and that matters of great interest may be occupying attention at headquarters and yet no information may reach them. If this represents any general feeling, is not the remedy to be found in wider and more earnest co-operation in our work on the part of the members generally ? The *Journal* of the Society was established to encourage this and to be an organ of communication between the members. I should be glad to see it more freely used for this purpose, and for the speedy publication of any first-hand evidence that our members may possess;

[1] In consequence of this appeal two members of the Society wrote to me that they would contribute £50 each if eighteen others would do the same so as to make up £1000 in the present year; £113 3s. has since been received, and perhaps some readers may feel moved to contribute towards the completion of the sum.

and also for the prompt communication of information from headquarters which would be of interest to members generally. I hope, therefore, without any departure from the caution and reserve, which are so necessary in dealing with the phenomena that engage our attention, we may be able to have a more frequent interchange of thought and opinion between the Council and the body of our members, and I shall be glad if I can be of any service in promoting this.

As regards wider co-operation in our work, I would venture to suggest *local groups* should be formed, meeting weekly or monthly for investigation or discussion.[1] If you ask me what work can be done by these local groups, a beginning might be made in the determination of two problems, which though they may be simple and dull, are nevertheless of considerable importance, and which can only be settled by wide-spread assistance.

One of these problems may be stated thus:

(1) Assuming the existence of telepathy, is the transference of thought from one person to another independently of the recognised channels of sensation, a faculty in some slight degree possessed *by all*, or is it confined only to a few? Prof. Richet and others have made experiments on this question, but it is still an open one. It is very easy to devise methods of experiments between two persons, choosing the simplest form, such as tossing a coin, and noting whether the right guesses in, say every 100 trials, somewhat exceed the number which chance alone would indicate. But patience is necessary in all investigations to make the result of any value, and also precautions with which no doubt you are familiar, such as the avoidance of facial or other indications. There are other questions in connection with telepathy which need elucidation to which I will refer presently.

The other problem is:

(2) To what extent is motor-automatism common among mankind? By motor automatism is meant the purposive movement of one's voluntary muscles without any intention or conscious effort on our part. The simplest and most sensitive

---

[1] No member of the Society has done more in this direction than Colonel Taylor, R.E., and I hope his example and admirable method of investigation will be widely followed.

test is to hold a forked twig in your hand after the manner of a dowser, and see if the twig curls up of its own accord when you walk round your garden, or go in search of some hidden object. Some one or more members of your investigating circle will probably succeed, in spite of their incredulity. Now it is important to know (1st) the percentage of success among all our friends, and (2nd) whether other phenomena of motor automatism occur with the same individual, such as the movement of the pendule explorateur, automatic writing, etc., and (3rd) whether these movements are merely fortuitous, or whether they are veridical, that is to say, do they give us truth-telling information of something the individual could not have ascertained by the use of his ordinary perceptive powers?

Now these problems require the willing co-operation of a number of intelligent investigators, but they do not require costly apparatus nor any particular training beyond that of careful observation; nor are these experiments in the least injurious to the operator, nor likely to excite any opposition even from a hyper-sensitive conscience. It is true they may seem trivial and tiresome: if any person think so, I am afraid they would think the details of all scientific investigation trivial and tiresome. The work of a bricklayer or a hodman in building a house would seem to be very monotonous, if we did not regard the end in view.

I am sometimes asked what our Society has already achieved, what has it done to justify its existence? The reply to this is found in the eighteen closely printed volumes of our *Proceedings*, and the eleven volumes of our *Journal*, containing an immense mass of evidence, the record of carefully sifted observations or of stringent experiments. These form a storehouse of material which we have every reason to believe will become increasingly valuable to students both of psychology and philosophy in the not distant future. Unquestionably a change of opinion is gradually coming about through the work of our Society. The widespread and unreasoning prejudice which 25 years ago existed against all psychical enquiry is breaking down. This is seen in the list of distinguished men who have become members of our society, and here I desire to welcome one of our great English savants, a man of European reputation, who has recently joined our ranks, and this coincidently with .his election to .the high position of joint Hon. Secretary to the Royal Society.

But although there is a more open mind on the part of science towards psychical research, it must be confessed it is still looked at somewhat askance by the leaders and organs of official science. It is worth a moment's attention to consider why this should be. No one asserts that the knowledge we are seeking to obtain is unimportant, for as the learned Dr. Glanville said 200 years ago about similar subjects to those we are studying, "These things relate to our biggest interests; if established they secure some of the outworks of religion." Nor, so far as I know, does any one assert we are hasty and incautious, or unscientific in our method of investigation. No doubt one reason for the present attitude of official science towards us has been the prevalence and paralysing influence of a materialistic philosophy, which denies the possibility of mind without a material brain, or of any means of access from other minds to our mind except through the recognised channels of sensation. Both these propositions are of course denied by our religious teachers, who assert that a spiritual world does exist, and that the inspired writings were given supersensuously to man. Nevertheless as a body, though with some notable exceptions, even *they* do not welcome us with open arms. The common ground and official view of both science and religion is that all extension to our existing knowledge in their respective departments can only come through the channels recognised by each; in the one case the channel is bounded by the five senses, and in the other case it is that sanctioned by authority. We must all admit that even unconsciously authority has a large share in moulding our convictions and determining our conduct, in fact we cannot emancipate ourselves from its subtle influence. As a rule this is beneficial, unless it can be shown that authority is untrustworthy; but the attempt to prove that it is so is sure to be an ungracious and difficult task, and almost certain to bring odium to bear upon those who, if they eventually prove to be right, are in a subsequent generation hailed as benefactors of the race.

Some years ago that most learned man, the late Prof. von

Helmholtz, visited Dublin. I had then recently published a paper giving for the first time *prima facie* evidence of something new to science, called thought-transference, now known as telepathy. Helmholtz, who was a great physiologist as well as physicist, had some conversation with me on the subject, and he ended by saying: " I cannot believe it. Neither the testimony of all the Fellows of the Royal Society, nor even the evidence of my own senses, would lead me to believe in the transmission of thought from one person to another independently of the recognised channels of sensation. It is clearly impossible." The respect that is due to so great a man renders it necessary to show in a few words why this statement (one that used to be common enough) is wholly indefensible. First, the phenomena in question, and all the phenomena within the scope of our Society, are not *contradictions*, but merely extensions of our existing knowledge ; they may be strange and inexplicable, but that merely indicates that the evidence in support of the new facts must be recognised as *adequate*. As Laplace long ago said in his *Theory of Probabilities*: " We are so far from knowing all the agents of nature, and their various modes of action, that it would not be philosophical to deny any phenomena merely because in the actual state of our knowledge they are inexplicable. This only ought we to do —in proportion to the difficulty there seems to be in admitting the facts should be the scrupulous attention we bestow on their examination."[1] That this is the true spirit may be seen from the recent discoveries in connection with Radium. These facts appeared even to contradict some of our previous knowledge. We always thought of an atom, as Lucretius did, "strong in solid singleness," as the most immutable and immortal thing in the physical universe. Now it appears to be capable of disintegration and transmutation, and the views of the alchemists are beginning to revive : soon we may be looking for the " philosopher's stone "—the substance that by its presence enables the transmutation of other heavy atoms to come about. Thus does the whirligig of time bring its revenges.

But to return. There is another fallacy in the scientific view expressed by Helmholtz. He said, as many do, that nothing could make him believe in such phenomena. But belief is not

[1] Laplace, *Théorie Analytique des Probabilités*, Introd., p. 43.

a voluntary act of the mind, it cannot be given or withheld at pleasure; it is, obviously, an involuntary state, which follows if our judgment considers the evidence adduced both adequate and conclusive. We can, of course, as many do, refuse to listen to the evidence; and it is worth noticing that in all our minds there is a tendency to repel the intrusion of any ideas unrelated to our usual habits of thought, and which therefore involve an uncomfortable dislocation of our mind: so that attention to evidence of this character is a difficult act of self-conquest. Hence every new departure in thought has to encounter great mental inertia, and wisely so, as preventing hasty and foolish aberrations of mind. But when attention is given, and the evidence considered adequate, it is sheer nonsense to say you won't believe it.

Is there then any other ground why science should not ungrudgingly recognise the evidence so amply given in our Proceedings? I have recently made enquiries among some of my scientific friends who stand aloof from us, to know what is their reason for so doing. Of course life is short, the claim of each particular branch of scientific investigation becomes increasingly exacting, and but few have time to consider the evidence. That is obvious, but why do they shrug their shoulders when you mention, say, telepathy, or the faculty of dowsing? Their attitude reminds me of an anecdote told by that remarkable woman, Miss Caroline Fox, and which I think is mentioned in the memorials of her life. The charming residence of Miss Fox in Cornwall was the meeting ground of many famous men of the last generation. On one occasion that great Irishman, Sir W. Rowan Hamilton, there met Sir G. Airy, the then Astronomer-Royal. Hamilton had just published his famous mathematical discovery of quaternions, and was, I believe, explaining it to Airy. After a short time Airy said, " I cannot see it at all." Hamilton replied, " I have been investigating the matter closely for many months, and I am certain of its truth." " Oh," rejoined Airy, " I have been thinking over it for the last two or three minutes, and there is nothing in it." This is why some of our scientific friends shrug their shoulders at our researches. They feel competent, after a few minutes' consideration, to reject conclusions which may have cost us years of investigation.

In fact, nine-tenths of the positive opinions we are accustomed to hear about psychical research are given *judicially*. That is, the objector speaks of his conclusions as positively as if it were his office to know the truth, and implies that any opposition is a thing for *him* to judge of. " He is annihilated," as Professor De Morgan pointed out some time ago, " by being reduced, no matter how courteously, from judge to counsel. But this is what must be done. The jurisdiction must be denied. The great art is not to pull him off the bench without ceremony, but to pull the bench from under him, without his exactly seeing how he came to tumble, and without proceeding to sit upon it yourself."

Enquiry among my scientific friends has shown me that the root of much, perhaps most, of the scientific scepticism towards our work is not because the phenomena are startling or inexplicable, but because they cannot be repeated at pleasure ; hence so very few scientific men have the opportunity of verifying the observations some of us have made. They do not doubt our good faith, but they think we may have been mistaken in our conclusions, and until we can reproduce the phenomena before them, they feel justified in distrusting our results. This might well give ground for suspense of judgment, but surely not for any hostile attitude. It is, of course, most desirable to be able to repeat our experiments at pleasure, but the very nature of our enquiry precludes this. We do not refuse to believe in the fall of meteoric stones unless we can see one falling. We may require a good deal of well-attested evidence for their fall, but, once the fact is established, the stringency of the evidence demanded immediately relaxes. Now, unquestionably there are at present more capable witnesses who can speak from personal and careful enquiry as to the fact of telepathy, or of what is called spiritualistic phenomena, than there are persons living who can testify to having seen the actual fall from space of meteoric stones.

The fact is, our scientific friends do not realise the profound difference that exists between the conditions of a physical and of a psychical experiment. We know what conditions are requisite in the former case, we do *not* know what they are in the latter, and hence the difficulty of all psychical investigation and the uncertainty of the reproduction of any given phenomenon.

A moment's consideration shows that the demand made upon us by science for the demonstration at any moment of a particular psychical phenomenon is inconsistent with the very object of our enquiry. Psychical experiments depend on the mental state of the subject; you may tell a person to do something, but whether he does it or not depends on the person addressed. Physical experiments are independent of our volition: a magnet attracts iron, or sets itself in the magnetic meridian, irrespective of our mental condition. This obvious difference between the two sets of phenomena is constantly overlooked. Physical science excludes from its survey the element of personality, with which we have to deal and over which we have little or no control. It regards all phenomena as strictly impersonal, and finds abundant field for investigation within the narrow limits it has marked out for itself: these things it regards as real, the rest as shadowy. The truth is, of course, exactly the reverse. The reality of which we are conscious is our self, our personality. It is the phenomena of external nature which are shadowy; shadows cast by some reality of which our senses tell us absolutely nothing.

There is, however, no reason why the methods so successfully pursued by science should not also be pursued in the study of the complex and shifting phenomena of human personality. Now this is precisely the object of our Society—the accurate investigation of that wide range of obscure but wonderful powers included within the mysterious thing we call ourself. Albeit we are but at the beginning of a task so vast that it may, in time to come, make all the discoveries of physical science seem trivial, all its labours seem insignificant in comparison with the stupendous problems that are before us.

We need, therefore, much more experimental evidence in every department of our work. So long ago as 1876, in a paper read before the British Association in that year, I stated that before science could attack with any hope of success the investigation of alleged spiritualistic phenomena, we must know whether definite ideas can unconsciously be communicated from one person to another: whether such a thing as thought-transference does really exist. Evidence was adduced in favour of this hypothesis. We have done much since then, but much remains to be done before telepathy can take its place as an accepted axiom of scientific knowledge.

I referred at the beginning of my address to some problems in connection with telepathy that await solution. Permit me for a few moments to return to this.

There is one question in regard to telepathy and similar psychical phenomena, which is likely to remain an outstanding difficulty. By what process can one mind affect another at a distance? Physical science teaches us that there is no such thing as "action at a distance." Energy at a distance reaches us either by the translation of matter through space, like a flying bullet, which carries the energy; or by the intermediary action of some medium, like the transmission of sound-bearing waves through the air, or of luminiferous waves through the ether, the energy being handed on from wave to wave. We may talk of brain waves, but that is only unscientific talk, we know of nothing of the kind. Neither do we know how gravitation acts across space: by what means such tremendous forces as bind the solar system together are either exerted or transmitted we know absolutely nothing. We don't talk of gravitation waves, we wait for further knowledge on this mysterious problem; and in like manner we must patiently wait for more light on the mode of transmission of thought through space. It may well be that thought transcends both matter and space, and has no relation to either. That mass, space, and time, may only be but the mental symbols we form of our present material system, and have no ultimate reality in themselves.

Another question is as follows: May not the uncertainty and difficulty of our experiments in thought-transference partly arise from the fact that we are not going to work the right way? We try to obtain evidence of the transmission of a word or idea through some conscious and voluntary act on the part of the percipient. We wait for a verbal or written response. Is not this a mistake? Ought we not rather to seek for evidence of thought-transference in the region of the sub-conscious life? I believe in the case of both the agent

and percipient the conscious will plays only a secondary part.
This is also true I think in all cases of suggestion, and of
the therapeutic effect of suggestion. It is notably seen in
the cures wrought by what is known as Christian Science.
I happen to have had occasion to study these somewhat
carefully of late, and undoubtedly remarkable cures are effected,
it may be by suggestion, but without the usual suggestive treatment; the only formula is the "Allness of God," and the
"non-existence of disease." But the healing processes are set
going by a purely sub-conscious act. And so in telepathy,
we need to hand over the whole matter to the subliminal
activities. The difficulty is how to do this. Hypnosis is
one way. And in the ordinary waking state, the agent, who
makes the suggestion, or transmits the idea, would I believe
do so more effectively if, after the intention had soaked into
his mind, he left it alone, so far as any conscious effort was
concerned. And the percipient should be as passive as
possible, make no effort to guess the word, but allow the
perception to reveal itself through some involuntary action.
Automatic writing would be the most effective, but that is
not very common; the twisting of the forked dowsing twig
might be utilised, indicating the letters of the alphabet by
its motion; or in other ways. In the historical researches I
have made on the so-called divining rod, I found it was used
in this very manner two centuries ago. In fact what we
need to learn is the language of the subliminal life, how it
speaks to us, how we can speak to it. The voluntary action
of the muscles in speech or gesture is the language of our
conscious life; the involuntary action of our muscles, and
emotional disturbance, appear to be the language of the sub-
conscious life.

Then another point should be noticed, the frequent *lagging*
of the impression in the percipient. I observed this again
and again in my first experiments in thought-transference 25
years ago. The correct reply to a previous experiment would
sometimes come in answer to a later and different experiment. I have noticed the same thing also in dowsing, with
some dowsers the motion of the twig lags behind the moment
of the impression; it turns *after* the dowser has passed a
little beyond the right spot. We have precisely similar phe-

nomena in physical science. The magnetic state of iron lags a little behind the magnetising force it is subjected to; this is known as *hysteresis*, from a Greek word signifying to lag behind. So I believe there is a psychical as well as a physical hysteresis, and if so, it should be reckoned with in our experiments. It is improbable that any psychical action, even of telepathy, occurs without some preceding change in the nerve tissues; in technical phraseology neurosis must always precede psychosis; and then this change must rise till it is of sufficient magnitude to create the reflex that moves the muscles. And all this involves time, which may be greater or less, and so account for the occasional lag we observe.

Other questions suggest themselves. Is it the idea or the word, the emotion or the expression of the emotion, that is transmitted in telepathy? Probably the idea. If so it affords a hint towards the interchange of thought amongst the race in spite of differences of language. Language is but a clumsy instrument of thought, and quite incommensurate to it; its arbitrary signs show it to be but the rudiments of a system which the evolutionary progress of the race may lead us to hope will be more perfect in the future. How much more accurately should we be able to transmit complex ideas and subtle emotions if thought could evoke thought without the mechanism of speech. This may now be the case in the state of life in the unseen. The sanctity and privacy of our minds will, however, require to be protected from unwelcome intrusion, and this, so far as our conscious life is concerned, will doubtless be within our own power to effect, so long as we retain control over our self-hood, our true personality.[1]

Then, again, may not animals share with man this telepathic power? They have in some directions keener perceptive faculties than man, and there is evidence that they are strongly affected by what we call apparitions. It may be that animals, and insects like the ant and the bee, *do* communicate with each other by some process analogous to telepathy. It is worth trying to find out whether say, a favourite dog can respond to a telepathic impact from his master. In centuries to come

---

[1] In that remarkable book published some 70 years ago, Isaac Taylor's *Physical Theory of Another Life*, Chap. viii., will be found a prevision of telepathy and of some of the ideas contained in the foregoing paragraph.

it is just possible that through some such interchange of feelings we may get into closer communion with all sentient things.

There is one argument in favour of the existence of something analogous to thought-transference, which—so far as I know—has not been used, and it is, I think, a legitimate argument, for it is based upon the underlying unity that exists throughout Nature. The theory of gravitation teaches us that every grain of sand on every seashore in this world, every particle of salt in every salt cellar, is for ever pulling every grain of sand or salt, not only on this earth, but on every planet, or star, in the whole Universe. And *vice versa*, for there is a reciprocal influence ever going on between these myriads of remote things. Nay, more, such is the solidarity of the Universe that an interchange of radiation, as well of attraction, is ever taking place between things on this earth, and also between our planet and every member of the solar system. No fact in physical science is more certain than this. May not this "theory of exchanges," this mobile equilibrium, extend to the psychical as well as the physical universe? Tennyson, with poetic prescience, asks in *Aylmer's Field*:

> "Star to star vibrates light, may soul to soul
> Strike thro' a finer element of her own?"

Certainly it seems very probable that every centre of consciousness is likely to react telepathically upon every other centre.[1]

[1] Since this address was delivered my attention has been drawn to Mrs. Browning's striking sonnet on "Life," wherein the same idea is elaborated; poets are certainly wonderful pioneers of thought; before telepathy was thought of Mrs. Browning wrote:

> "Each creature holds an insular point in space;
> Yet what man stirs a finger, breathes a sound,
> But all the multitudinous beings round
> In all the countless worlds, with time and place
> For their conditions, down to the central base,
> Thrill, haply, in vibration and rebound,
> Life answering life across the vast profound,
> In full antiphony, by a common grace?
> I think this sudden joyaunce which illumes
> A child's mouth sleeping, unaware may run
> From some soul newly loosened from earth's tombs:
> I think this passionate sigh, which half begun
> I stifle back, may reach and stir the plumes
> Of God's calm angel standing in the sun."

It is hard to believe that the play of *vital* forces should be more restricted than that of the *physical* forces; that radio-activities should be confined to inanimate matter. If this unconscious radiation and reaction is going on between mind and mind, then observed cases of telepathy would simply mean the awakening of consciousness to the fact in certain minds. Why some and not all minds, and why so fitfully the conscious perception should be aroused, are problems we must leave to the future, they are quite consistent with what we find everywhere in nature. For my own part, I am disposed to think this inter-change is common to the race, and is the chief reason why all men are insensibly moulded by their environment. Only, as I said just now, I believe the telepathic exchange emanates from and affects the sub-conscious part of our personality. It is potentially conscious, and may, and probably will eventually become an integral part of our self-consciousness.

We know as a matter of fact that a vast number of im-pressions are constantly being made upon us, of which we take no heed; they do not interest us, or they are not strong enough to arouse consciousness. But the impressions are *there*, they leave a mark upon us though we are not aware of it, and they may float to the surface, or be evoked at some future time. One of the most certain and striking results of the investigations made by our Society is that the content of our sub-conscious life is far greater than that of our conscious life. Our minds are like a photographic plate, sensitive to all sorts of im-pressions, but our ego develops only a few of these impressions, these are our conscious perceptions, the rest are latent, awaiting development, which may come in sleep, hypnosis, or trance, or by the shock of death, or after death.

But even here and now this sub-conscious radio-activity of thought may already play some part in the growing sense of sympathy and humanity we find in the race. And what a change would be wrought if it were suddenly to become an element of consciousness among mankind. To realise the brother-hood of the race would not then be a pious aspiration or a strenuous effort, but *the* reality of all others most vividly before us; involuntarily sharers in one another's pleasures and pains, the welfare of our fellow-men would be *the* factor in our lives which would dominate all our conduct. What would be the use of a luxurious club and Parisian cooks if the privation and suffering of the destitute were telepathically part and parcel of our lives? Slowly the race *does* seem to be awakening to the sense of a larger self, which embraces the many in the One, to

> "A heart that beats
> In all its pulses with the common heart
> Of humankind, which the same things make glad,
> The same make sorry."

The instinct of true religion, like the insight of the true poet, arrives at some great verity without the process of reasoning or the need of proof. Thus it has been with the belief in prayer and in the efficacy of prayer. Scepticism scoffs at a mystery which involves the direct action of mind on mind and the still greater mystery of the movement of the Infinite by the finite,— but faith remains unshaken. For us wayfaring men, however, reason needs some help in climbing the steeps attained by faith. And is not this help afforded by the steps slowly being cut in the upward path by means of psychical research? What is telepathy but the proof of the reasonableness of prayer? No longer need our reason rest content with the plausible explanation that prayer can do no more than evoke a subjective response in the suppliant, that it is inconceivable how the Infinite and the finite mind, the One manifest in the many, can have any community of thought. On the contrary, if telepathy be indisputable, if our creaturely minds can, without voice or sensation, impress each other, the Infinite mind is likely thus to have revealed itself in all ages to responsive human hearts. Some may have the spiritual ear, the open vision, but to all of us there comes at times the echo of that larger Life which is slowly expressing itself in humanity as the ages gradually unfold. In fact the teaching of science has ever been that we are not isolated in, or from, the great Cosmos; the light of suns and stars reaches us, the mysterious force of gravitation binds the whole material universe into an organic whole, the minutest molecule and the most distant orb are bathed in one and the self-same medium. But surely beyond and above all these material links is the solidarity of Mind. As the essential significance and unity of a honeycomb is not in the cells of wax, but in the common life and purpose of the builders of those cells, so the true significance of nature is not in the material world but in the Mind that gives to it a meaning, and that underlies and unites, that transcends and creates, the phenomenal world through which for a moment each of us is passing. "The things which are seen are temporal, but the things which are unseen are eternal."

I will now turn for a few minutes to another branch of our researches, which has special interest for me as it was this subject that first aroused my interest in experimental psychology and to which I gave many months of experiment long before our Society was founded. I refer to Hypnotism.

There are no doubt many present who remember the outcry that was once raised against the investigation of hypnotism, then called mesmerism. Constant attacks were made by the medical and scientific world on the one hand, and by the religious world on the other, upon the early workers at this subject. They were denounced as impostors, shunned as pariahs, and unceremoniously pitched out of the synagogues both of science and religion ; and this within my own memory. Physiological and medical science can only hang its head in shame when it looks back upon that period. What do we find to-day—the subject of hypnotism and its therapeutic value recognised ! It has now become an integral part of scientific teaching and investigation in several medical schools, more especially on the Continent. I think our Society may fairly lay claim to have contributed to this change of view, and the work of our members, Edmund Gurney, and Doctors Arthur Myers, Milne Bramwell and Lloyd Tuckey, has added much to the knowledge of a subject the importance of which it is difficult to overrate. It is also worthy of note how the former neglect of this subject by science relegated it to the ignorant and the charlatan, and its practice to mysterious and often mischievous public amusements. These are now less common ; and though the public apprehension of the dangerous abuse of hypnotism is grossly exaggerated, for it is less open to abuse than chloroform, I, for one, am strongly of opinion that we, as a Society, should discourage, and (as in many Continental countries) get the legislature to forbid the practice of hypnotism except under proper medical supervision.

Now I think it is the duty of our Society to cherish the memory of these courageous seekers after truth, who were the pioneers in this and other branches of psychical research. The splendid and self-sacrificing labours of those distinguished physicians, Doctors Elliotson and Esdaile, in the fields of hypnotic therapeutics and painless surgery under hypnosis should never be forgotten, any more than the later work of Dr. Braid of Manchester. Dr. Elliotson, though at the head of his profession, sacrificed everything for the advancement of this branch of knowledge. The mesmeric hospital in London, and the similar hospital founded in Calcutta by an enlightened Governor-General and placed under the care of Dr. Esdaile, did remarkable work, too little known at the present day. I am therefore glad to see in Dr. Milne Bramwell's *magnum opus* on hypnotism that he draws special attention to the labours of Elliotson, Esdaile and Braid. And it is to be regretted how completely these pioneers are ignored in the works on suggestive therapeutics by Dr. Bernheim, Dr. Liébeault, Dr. Schofield, and some others.

Leaving this part of our subject, now within the purview of science, let us pass to the extreme or advanced wing of psychical research; to that part of our work on which considerable differences of opinion exist even within our Society. I refer to spiritualistic phenomena. With regard to these we must all agree that indiscriminate condemnation on the one hand, and ignorant credulity on the other, are the two most mischievous elements with which we are confronted in connection with this subject. It is because we, as a Society, feel that in the fearless pursuit of truth it is the paramount duty of science to lead the way, that the scornful attitude of the scientific world towards even the investigation of these phenomena is so much to be deprecated. Hence, as in the case of those who were the pioneers in the study of hypnotism, we ought not to forget the small band of investigators who before our time had the courage, after patient enquiry, to announce their belief in what, for want of any better theory, they called spiritualistic phenomena. No doubt we can pick holes in their method of investigation, but they were just as honest, just as earnest seekers after truth, as we claim to be, and they deserve more credit than we can lay claim to, for they had to encounter greater opposition and vituperation. The superior person then, as now, smiled at the credulity of those better informed than himself. I suppose we are all apt to fancy our own power of discernment and of sound judgment to be somewhat better than our neighbours'. But after all is it not the common-sense, the care, the patience, and the amount of uninterrupted attention we bestow upon any psychical phenomena we are investigating, that gives value to the opinion at which we arrive, and not the particular cleverness or scepticism of the observer? The lesson we all need to learn is that what even the humblest of men *affirm* from their own experience, is always worth listening to, but what even the cleverest of men, in their ignorance, *deny* is never worth a moment's attention.

The acute and powerful intellect of Professor De Morgan, the great exposer of scientific humbug, long ago said, and he had the courage publicly to state, that however much the Spiritualists might be ridiculed, they were undoubtedly on the track that has led to all advancement in knowledge, for they had the *spirit* and *method* of the old times, when paths had to be cut through the uncleared forests in which we can now easily walk.[1] Their *spirit* was that of universal examination unchecked by the fear of being detected in the investigation of nonsense. This was the spirit that animated the Florentine Academicians and the first Fellows of the Royal Society 250 years ago; they set to work to prove all things that they might hold fast to that which was good. And their *method* was that of all scientific research, viz., to start a theory and see how it worked. Without a theory "facts are a mob, not an army." Meteorology at the present moment is buried under a vast mob of observations for want of ingenuity in devising theories; *any* working hypothesis is better than none at all. And so I agree with De Morgan that the most sane and scientific method in psychical research is not to be afraid of propounding a theory because it may seem extraordinary, but have courage to do so and see if it works. The theory of thought-transference led to the accumulation of evidence which

[1] See Preface of *From Matter to Spirit*, p. xviii.

bids fair, sooner or later, to place telepathy among the established truths of science.

The amusing feature in the progress of knowledge is that, usually, critics who resist as long as they can a new theory are apt afterwards, when the theory becomes widely accepted, to use it indiscriminately, as if it covered all obscure phenomena; and so it becomes a kind of fetish in their thoughts. We are all familiar with the imposture theory, with the coincidence theory, and with the telepathic theory; each excellent in their way, but most foolish and unscientific if we allow any one of them to obscure our vision or paralyse our investigation. What is to be reprobated, as De Morgan said, "is not the wariness which widens and lengthens enquiry, but the *assumption* which prevents and narrows it."

Instances are well known of the most acute and careful enquirers, trained psychical detectives we might call them, who having begun with *a priori* reasoning and resolute scepticism, when they have thrown aside their preconceived assumptions, and given the necessary time and patience to the investigation of one particular case, have gone over to the spiritualistic camp. They may be right or wrong in their present opinion, but we must all admit they have far better reasons for forming a judgment than any of us can have. If they are right it follows that the particular case they have investigated is not likely to be a solitary one, but typical of similar cases with us as well as with them.

Pray do not suppose I hold a brief on behalf of spiritualism either as a practice or a religion. On the contrary, to my mind few things are more dismal than the common run of spiritualistic séances. Sometimes they revolt one's feelings, and always they are a weariness to the flesh. Perhaps the manifold experiences I have had have been unfortunate, and I freely admit my remarks apply more particularly to sittings with professional mediums, where what are called physical manifestations take place, which always seem to be on a lower plane, even where the possibility of fraud has been carefully excluded. Nevertheless, if we can get at truth, what does it matter whether we draw it from a well or drag it from a bog?

It is impossible, however, not to feel some sympathy with

the common objection of the doubter that the phenomena are of so paltry a character. But we cannot prescribe to nature, we cannot get rid of the leprosy of doubt by choosing rivers of our own to wash in. And so we must be content with what we find. After all, from a scientific point of view, *nothing* can be paltry or mean that manfests *life*.

Bacteriologists spend their days searching for evidence of the lowest forms of life. And surely any evidence of personality that gives us the faintest, rudest sign that life still persists though the clothing of the body be gone, is worth infinite trouble to attain. Though it may be

"Only a signal shown and a voice from out of the darkness,"

it is not paltry. In fine, it is this natural human longing that renders a dispassionate consideration of the facts, a calm and critical weighing of the evidence, so difficult and yet so imperative.

We must, however, bear in mind, as was pointed out by the present Prime Minister in the remarkable address he delivered from this chair, that if science had first attempted to include in its survey not only physical but psychical phenomena it might for centuries have lost itself in dark and difficult regions, and the work of science to-day would then have been *less*, not more complete.[1] This is very true, the foundations of our faith in the undeviating order of nature had to be laid by the investigation of the laws of matter and motion and by the discovery of the orderly evolution of life. What science has now established is that the universe is a cosmos, not a chaos, that amidst the mutability of all things there is no capriciousness, no disorder ; that in the interpretation of nature, however entangled or obscure the phenomena may be, we shall never be put to intellectual confusion.

Now, if instead of investigating the normal phenomena of the world in which we live, science had first grappled with supernormal phenomena, it would not have reached so soon its present assured belief in a reign of law. We believe that fuller knowledge of the obscure phenomena we are investigating will in time come to us, as it has in other branches of

[1] *Proceedings* S.P.R., vol. x., p. 5.

science, but the appearances are so elusive, the causes so complex, the results of work sometimes so disheartening, that we need the steadying influence of the habit of thought engendered by science to enable us patiently and hopefully to pursue our way.

Possibly historical research amongst the most ancient records may give us fragments of unsuspected information ; for it is very probable that many, if not all the psychical phenomena we are now investigating were known, and the knowledge jealously guarded, in ages long past. The very high civilisation which is now known to have existed thousands of years before Christ in the earliest Egyptian dynasties, makes it almost inconceivable to imagine that subjects of such transcendent interest to mankind were not then part of the learning of the few, part of " the wisdom of Egypt." The seizure of this knowledge by the priestly caste and its restriction to themselves, with penalties to all intruders, was the natural sequence of the lower civilisation that followed. Thus psychical phenomena became veiled in mystery, and ultimately degraded to a mischievous superstition. Mystic rites were added to impress the multitude; finally divination, enchantment, augury, and necromancy became methods of wielding a mysterious power held by the few. But such practices " wearied the people's intellect, destroyed their enterprise and distorted their conscience." [1] The industry and politics of the people became paralysed by giving heed to an oracle, or to gibbering spirits, rather than to reason and strenuous endeavour. The great Hebrew prophets, the statesmen of their day, saw this clearly and had the courage to denounce such practices in unmistakable terms; warning the people that by using these things as an infallible guide, or as a religion, they were being misled, and reason was being dethroned from her seat. And so the burden of their speech was, " Thy spells and enchantments with which thou hast wearied thyself have led thee astray." [2] Hence these practices were prohibited, as a careful study of the whole subject shows, because they enervated the nation, and tended to obscure the Divine idea; to weaken the supreme faith in, and reverent worship of, the one omnipotent Being the Hebrew

[1] Prof. G. A. Smith in his brilliant and scholarly work on Isaiah, vol. 2., p. 199.
[2] Cf. latter half of Isaiah, 47 ch.

nation was set apart to proclaim. With no assured knowledge of the great world-order we now possess, these elusive occult phenomena confused both the intellectual and moral sense, and so they were wisely thrust aside. But the danger at the present day is very different. Instead of a universe peopled with unseen personalities, the science of to-day has gone to the other extreme, and as Mr. Myers once eloquently said, we are now taught to believe "the Universe to be a soulless interaction of atoms, and life a paltry misery closed in the grave." Were the Hebrew prophets now amongst us, surely their voice would not be raised in condemnation of the attempts we are making to show that the order of Nature contains an even vaster procession of phenomena than are now embraced within the limits of recognised science, and that behind the appearances with which science deals there are more enduring and transcendent realities.

I have ventured upon this digression in the hope that I may remove the misgivings with which a part of our work is regarded by some leaders of religious opinion, who from time to time have been in communication with me. Perhaps I may also add that the aversion which some feel towards any enquiry into spiritualistic phenomena arises I think from a misapprehension. With what is spiritual, with religion, these phenomena have nothing in common. They may afford us a rational belief in the existence of life without a visible body, of thought without material protoplasm, and so become the handmaid of faith. But they belong to a wholly different order from that of religious faith. Our concern is solely with the evidence for certain *phenomena*; and as Professor Karl Pearson has said, "Wherever there is the slightest possibility for the mind of men to *know*, there is a legitimate problem for science." Hence *all* appearances, whether of microbes or of men, are legitimate subjects of investigation. Because they happen to be fitful, or phenomena occurring in an unseen environment, does not render the investigation improper or unscientific, though it makes it considerably more difficult.

Now the investigations we have published undeniably establish the fact, that human personality embraces a far larger scope than science has hitherto recognised. That it partakes of a *two-fold life*, on one side a self-consciousness which is awakened by, and related to time and space, to sense and outward things; on the other side a deeper, slumbering, but potential consciousness, the record of every unheeded past impression, possessing higher receptive and perceptive powers than our normal self-consciousness, a self that, I believe, links our individual life to the ocean of life, and to the Source of all life. It is a remarkable fact that long ago the philosopher Kant instinctively stated the same truth. He says: "[It is possible that] the human soul even in this life stands in indissoluble community with all immaterial natures of the spirit world, it mutually acts upon them and receives from them impressions, of which, however, as man, it is unconscious as long as all goes well." [1] This, of course, was Swedenborg's view. He frequently tells us, "Man is so constituted that he is at the *same time* in the spiritual world and in the natural world." Plotinus, who lived in the third century, held a similar belief, this was in fact the view of the Neo-Platonists and of the later mystics generally.[2] In connection with this subject may I commend to you the perusal of Dr. Du Prel's *Philosophy of Mysticism*, which has been translated with loving labour by one of the earliest and best friends of our Society, Mr. C. C. Massey: perhaps the most valuable part of the work being the suggestive introduction which Mr. Massey has himself added.[3]

[1] "Es wird künftig, ich weiss nicht wo oder wann, noch bewiesen werden, dass die menschliche Seele auch in diesen Leben in einer unauflöslich verknüpften Gemeinschaft mit allen immateriellen Naturen der Geisterwelt stehe, dass sie wechselweise in diese wirke und von ihnen Eindrücke empfange, deren sie sich als Mensch nicht bewusst ist, so lange alles wohl steht." (Kant's *Sammtliche Werke*, Hartenstein's Edition, 1867, vol. ii., p. 341.)

[2] Vaughan's "Hours with the Mystics," vol. i., contains an excellent summary of the views of the Neo-Platonists. Philo Judæus writing from Alexandria a few years B.C. says, "This alliance with an upper world, of which we are conscious, would be impossible, were not the soul of man an indivisible portion of the divine and blessed spirit." See also Thomas Taylor's translation of some of the works of Plotinus.

[3] Here perhaps I may add one line expressive of my own indebtedness to and affectionate regard for my dear friend C. C. Massey, whose knowledge of all that relates to the higher problems before our Society is more profound than that of any one I know.

There is one interesting point in connection with spiritualistic phenomena which is worth a little attention. As we are all aware, the production of these phenomena appears to be inseparably connected with some special person whom we call "mediumistic." This fact affords perennial amusement to the man in the street. But from a purely scientific standpoint there is nothing remarkable in this. Recent discoveries have revealed the fact that a comparatively few substances possess what is called radio-active power. Unlike ordinary forms of matter, these radio-active bodies possess an inherent and peculiar structure of their own. There is therefore nothing absurd in supposing that there may be a comparatively few persons who have a peculiar and remarkable mental structure differing from the rest of mankind. Moreover, the pathologist or alienist does not refuse to investigate epilepsy or monomania because restricted to a limited number of human beings.

Furthermore, physical science gives us abundant analogies of the necessity of some *intermediary* between the unseen and the seen. Waves in the luminiferous ether require a material medium to absorb them before they can be perceived by our senses. The intermediary may be a photographic plate, a fluorescent screen, the retina, a black surface, or an electric resonator, according to the length of those waves. But some medium formed of ponderable matter is absolutely necessary to render the actinic, luminous, thermal, or electrical effects of these waves perceptible to our senses. And the more or less perfect rendering of the invisible waves depends on the more or less perfect synchronism between the unseen motions of the ether and the response of the material medium that absorbs and manifests them.

Thus we find certain definite physical media are necessary to enable operations to become perceptible which otherwise remain imperceptible. Through these media energy traversing the unseen is thereby arrested, and, passing through ponderable matter, is able to affect our senses and arouse consciousness.

Now, the nexus between the seen and the unseen may be physical or psychical, but it is always a specialised substance, or living organism. In some cases the receiver is a body in a state of unstable equilibrium, a sensitive material—like one of Sir Oliver Lodge's receivers for wireless telegraphy—and in that case its behaviour and idiosyncrasies need to be studied beforehand. It is doubtless a peculiar psychical state, of the nature of which we know nothing, that enables certain persons whom we call mediums to act as receivers, or resonators, through which an unseen intelligence can manifest itself to us. And this receptive state is probably a sensitive condition easily affected by its mental environment.

We should not go to a photographer who took no trouble to protect his plates·from careless exposure before putting them in the camera. And I do not know why we should expect anything but a confused result from a so-called medium (or automatist, as Myers suggested they should be called) if the mental state of those present reacts unfavourably upon the sensitive. Infinite patience and laborious care in observation we must have (as in all difficult investigation), but what good results from any scientific research could we expect if we started with the presumption that there was nothing to investigate but imposture ?

In connection with this subject of mediumship, it seems to me very probable that a medium, an intermediary of some sort, is not only required on our side in the seen, but is also required *on the other side* in the unseen. In all communication of thought from one person to another a double translation is necessary. Thought, in some inscrutable way, acts. upon the medium of our brain, and becomes expressed in written or spoken words. These words, after passing through space, have again to be translated back to thought through the medium of another brain. That is to say, there is a descent from thought to gross matter on one side, a transmission through space, and an ascent from gross matter to thought on the other side. Now, the so-called medium, or automatist, acts as *our* brain, translating for us the impressions made upon it and which it receives across space from the unseen. But there must be a corresponding descent of thought on the other side to such a telepathic form that it can act upon the material particles of the brain of our medium. It may be even more difficult to find a spirit medium there· than here. No doubt wisely so, for the invasion of our consciousness here might otherwise be so frequent and troublesome as to paralyse the conduct of our life. It is possible therefore that much of the difficulty and confusion of the manifestations which are recorded in our *Proceedings*, and in the very valuable contribution which Mr. Piddington has just given us of sittings with Mrs. Thompson, are due to inevitable difficulties in translation on *both* sides?[1]

Furthermore, if my view be correct, that the self-conscious part of our personality plays but a subordinate part in any telepathic transmission, whether from incarnate or discarnate minds, we shall realise how enormously complex the problem becomes. So that the real person whom we knew on earth may find the difficulty of self-manifestion too great to overcome, and only a fitful fragment of their thoughts can thus reach us.

There is, however, another view of the matter which to me seems very probable. The transition from this life to the next may in some respects resemble our ordinary awakening from sleep. The discarnate soul not improbably regards the circumstances of his past life "in this dream-world of ours," as we now regard a dream upon awakening. If, even immediately upon awakening, we try to recall all the incidents of a more or less vivid dream, we find how difficult it is to do so, how fragmentary the whole appears; and yet in some way we are conscious the dream was a far more coherent and real thing than we can express in our waking moments. Is it not a frequent and provoking experience that whilst some trivial features recur to us, the dream as a whole is elusive, and as time passes on even the most vivid dream is gone beyond recall? May it not be that something analogous to this awaits us when we find ourselves amid the transcendent realities of the unseen universe? The deep impress of the present life will doubtless be left on our personality, but its details may be difficult to bring into consciousness, and we may

---

[1] Miss Jane Barlow, who has made a close study of these communications, writes to me on this point: "The almost unimaginable difficulty in communicating may account for many of the failures, mistakes, and absurdities we notice. I think we are apt to lay too much stress on the want of memory. Apart from purely evidential considerations, there seems a tendency to regard it as a larger and more essential element of Personality than it really is. In my own case, for instance, any trivial cause—a headache, a cold, or a little flurry—scatters my memory for proper names. I can easily imagine myself forgetting my own name without suffering from any serious confusion of intellect in other respects, or the least decay of personality."

find them fading from us as we wake to the dawn of the eternal day.

Whatever view we take, the records of these manifestations in our *Proceedings* give us the impression of a truncated personality, "the dwindling remnant of a life," rather than of a fuller, larger life. Hence, whilst in my opinion psychical research *does show us* that intelligence can exist in the unseen, and personality can survive the shock of death, we must not confuse mere, and perhaps temporary, survival after death with that higher and more expanded life which we desire and mean by immortality, and the attainment of which, whatever may be our creed, is only to be won through the "process of the Cross." For it is by self-surrender, the surrender, that is, of all that fetters "What we feel within ourselves is highest," that we enter the pathway of self-realisation. Or as Tennyson expresses it :—

> "Thro' loss of Self
> The gain of such large life as match'd with ours
> Were Sun to spark—unshadowable in words,
> Themselves but shadows of a shadow-world." [1]

[1] So also Goethe :

> "Und so lang du das nicht hast
> Dieses : 'stirb und werde' !
> Bist du nur ein trüber gast
> Auf der dunken Erde."

which a friend has rendered as follows :

> "Whoso heeds not this behest
> 'Die to win new birth,'
> Lives but as a hapless guest
> On a darkening earth."

SOME REMINISCENCES OF FIFTY YEARS' PSYCHICAL RESEARCH.[1]

" Science is bound by the everlasting law of honour to face fearlessly every problem that can fairly be presented to it."—LORD KELVIN.

JUST fifty years ago this month I first began a serious and systematic investigation of psychical phenomena, and was so impressed with the supreme importance of the subject that so far as my time and strength permitted I have continued the investigation to the present time with unabated interest. Of course, other and far abler men both preceded me and worked contemporaneously with me ; to some of these I will refer directly.

EARLY PSYCHICAL RESEARCHERS.

By psychical research I mean the critical investigation, and, where possible, the verification of alleged supernormal phenomena, or of hitherto unrecognised human faculties.

So far as regards narratives of spiritistic phenomena, these of course go back to remote ages, and records are to be found in many different countries. Years ago Andrew Lang had several conversations with me on the value of the S.P.R. devoting some time to historical research on this subject, for he attached great importance to the fact of the wide diffusion, both in space and time, of phenomena similar to those we are now engaged in investigating.[2]

---

[1] Read at a Private Meeting of the Society on June 17, 1924.

[2] The laborious and admirable work by William Howitt, entitled *History of the Supernatural*, is well known and should be consulted by all who are interested in the history of psychical research. It made a great impression on me when I read it some fifty years ago. The term *supernatural* should, however, have been *supernormal*, as all phenomena—however novel and inexplicable they may appear to be—are really *natural* ; only God is above and beyond Nature.

Biblical references show that Spiritualism was rampant in the early history of the Jews ; King Saul himself being a notable spiritualist, consulting his medium at Endor. As I have said elsewhere, before science had established a universal reign of law or of the great world order, the pursuit of these spiritistic phenomena was justly, condemned by the ancient prophets as likely to lead to intellectual and moral confusion. It seems probable, however, that many of the prophetic writings were done automatically, as in the book of *Chronicles* David says that the instructions he gave regarding the building of the Temple were not his own ideas, for "the Lord made me understand in writing *by his hand upon me*."[1]

One of the first psychical researchers of whom I can find any report was the learned and famous German Jesuit, Fr. A. Kircher. In his Latin folios, published in 1640, he discusses the cause of the motion of the 'pendule explorateur' (a little ball or ring suspended by a string held by one hand) and of the forked divining rod, both of which at that time were the subject of acute controversy. Kircher showed that if the 'pendule' or the rod were held, not by the hand, but by a rigid support, no motion occurs under any circumstances. He was thus led to discover the principle of unconscious muscular action, a discovery claimed two centuries later by the distinguished French chemist, Chevreul, and by Dr. W. B. Carpenter subsequently.

Some twenty years after Kircher's work appeared, one of the founders of the Royal Society, the Hon. Robert Boyle, 'the son of the Earl of Cork and the Father of Chemistry,' in his *Philosophical Works* discusses the question of the divining rod, and urges further experiments to test its value in the discovery of mineral veins, for the evidence he collected was conflicting. He remarks that eye-witnesses, who were far from credulous, told him of the great value of the rod, and one gentleman in whose hand it moved when he passed over a vein of ore, affirmed "that the motion of his hand did not at all contribute to the inclination of the rod, but that sometimes when

[1] See 1 *Chron.* xxviii. 19.

he held it very fast it would bend so strongly as to break in his hand." [1]

In one of the first volumes of the *Philosophical Transactions of the Royal Society* Boyle asks the question whether anyone could inform him "whether diggers do meet with the subterraneous demons which are said to inhabit the lead mines of Somersetshire, and in what shape and manner they appear ? " In a subsequent number the famous Dr. Glanvil, also a Fellow of the Royal Society, replied that he lived near the lead mines in the Mendips, and that whilst the miners heard the knockings of the demons, and by following the directions of these knockings were led to plenty of ore, nevertheless he had not found anyone who had actually *seen* the demons or gnomes themselves, and therefore he could not describe their appearance or habits.[2] A curious fact is that these knockings are heard and the gnomes believed in by lead miners in various parts of England and Ireland. The simple scientific explanation of these sounds I think I have discovered, but it would take me too far to go into the matter here. The point I want to bring out is that Boyle and Glanvil and many of the early Fellows of the Royal Society were true psychical researchers ; as Prof. de Morgan has said, "they set themselves to work to prove all things, that they might hold fast to that which was good ; they bent themselves to the question whether sprats were young herrings and whether a spider could crawl through the powder of a unicorn's horn." They enquired whether there was any value in magnetical cures and any good in Kenelm Digby's sympathetic powder. Even a century later the great Sir Isaac Newton describes in a series of letters—which I have seen, as they have been preserved by my friend, Mr. Blayny Balfour—how he spent much time and money in testing the value of certain alchemical powders which were said to turn lead into gold.

The early spiritualists really took the method of these pioneers of physical science. Though they might have

---

[1] Boyle's *Philosophical Works* (1738), vol. i., p. 172 and 173.

[2] *Phil. Trans.*, No. 19, Nov. 1666 ; and Glanvil's reply is in *Phil. Trans.*, vol. iii., 1668.

been frequently too credulous, yet what they aimed at was to collect facts however improbable they appeared to be, and as De Morgan says, "The spiritualists beyond a doubt are in the track that has led to all advancement in physical science; they have the spirit and the method of the grand time when paths had to be cut through the uncleared forests in which it is now the daily routine to walk. Their spirit was that of universal examination, wholly unchecked by fear of being discovered in the investigation of nonsense." [1]

One of the earliest Fellows of the Royal Society, to whom I have already referred, was Dr. Joseph Glanvil; he was chaplain to Charles II. and a prebendary of Worcester. The historian Lecky describes him as "a man of incomparable ability." Speaking of one of Glanvil's works, Lecky remarks, "it would be difficult to find a work displaying less of credulity and superstition than this treatise." Glanvil's *Saducismus Triumphatus*, published at the end of the seventeenth century, discusses the evidence concerning witches and apparitions, and gives the fullest report of those remarkable poltergeist phenomena known as the 'Demon of Tedworth' or the "Disturbances in Mr. Mompesson's house in Wiltshire." Glanvil truly remarks that "matters of fact well proved ought not to be denied because we cannot conceive how they could be performed. Deceit and fallacy will only warrant a greater care and caution in examining." Glanvil had the warm support not only of Robert Boyle, but also of the famous Henry More.

In his record of the hauntings of the Epworth parsonage in 1716, and in his endeavour to get first-hand evidence of other supernormal phenomena, John Wesley—as Mr. J. Arthur Hill has said—"would have made an excellent member of the S.P.R.," and it is certainly surprising—as Mr. Hill adds—"to find in an earnestly religious man of that day, such as John Wesley, so much critical interest in our subject."

Coming to more recent times, the memoir of the eleventh Duke of Somerset, the great grandfather of our friend and

[1] Preface to *From Matter to Spirit*, pp. 18-20.

fellow-worker, Miss Ramsden, shows that the Duke was really a keen psychical researcher, for he critically examined several psychic cases, among others the well-known dream of a Cornish farmer, Williams, who on May 11, 1812, woke his wife and told her that he had dreamt he had seen a man shot in the lobby of the House of Commons, and described his appearance, etc. The dream was repeated, and told to several people; subsequently it was found that the details of the dream exactly corresponded with the facts connected with the assassination of Mr. Percival, the Chancellor of the Exchequer, on the eleventh May, the very evening Williams had his dream.[1] Percival's descendant—my venerable friend, Miss Percival of Chobham—has also given me a written contemporary record of this remarkable dream.

Among the Fellows of the Royal Society who warmly advocated the investigation of psychical phenomena, was Dr. Mayo, F.R.S., Professor of Physiology in King's College, London, whose writings on the subject, published about the middle of the last century, are well worth perusal, containing as they do many new and interesting facts, which at the present day seem little known.

This period was also notable for the great interest excited by mesmeric phenomena. The remarkable report of the committee appointed by the medical section of the French Academy of Sciences on this subject, together with the amazing phenomena to which they testify, excited widespread interest. Eminent English physicians and surgeons, such as Dr. Elliotson of St. Thomas' Hospital and Dr. Esdaile, presidency surgeon in Calcutta, made numerous contributions to our knowledge on this subject, especially as regards the therapeutic and analgesic power of mesmerism. Esdaile, as is well known, conducted a very large number of *major* surgical operations, absolutely painlessly, under the mesmeric trance; and if the use of chloroform as an anaesthetic had not been discovered about this time, the value of mesmeric trance in surgical operations would have been universally acknowledged. But

[1] See p. 335 in Lady Gwendolen Ramsden's *Correspondence of Two Brothers from 1809-1819* (Longmans & Co.).

in spite of the eminence of Dr. Elliotson and others, mesmerism was nevertheless denounced by the profession as a whole, and the *Lancet* called it "an odious fraud." It was not until Braid of Manchester employed the word *hypnotism* instead of mesmerism—and thus dissociated the subject from Mesmer, who was more or less of a quack—that the medical profession began to treat the subject with less contempt. Braid also gave a reasonable explanation of the phenomena, but subsequently this proved to be inadequate to account for all the facts. The valuable experimental work of the continental hypnotists, and of our own members, Edmund Gurney, Dr. Lloyd Tuckey and Dr. Milne Bramwell, have now placed hypnotic treatment among the recognised therapeutic agencies of the medical profession.

FOUNDATION OF THE SOCIETY FOR PSYCHICAL RESEARCH.

Some twenty-five years before our Society was founded a few of the younger Fellows of Trinity College, Cambridge, chief of whom was Mr. B. F. Westcott—afterwards the famous Bishop of Durham—started a ' Ghost Society ' very much on the lines of our S.P.R.   In our *Journal* for April last year I gave the object and the brief history of this Society, which included among its members several Cambridge graduates who subsequently became eminent, such as Archbishop Benson, Prof. Henry Sidgwick, and others. I will hand over for preservation among the archives of our Society the original document of the ' Cambridge Ghost Club ' (as it was called), given to me by my friend the Archdeacon of Dublin.

As regards the foundation of our own Society, I have corrected elsewhere the misunderstanding which Prof. Richet and others have fallen into ; [1] and also I wrote, by request, a fuller account of the early history of our Society.[2]   Though it is true I happened to be the chief instrument in the foundation of our Society in 1882—and of kindred societies in Canada and the United States in

[1] See *Journal of the S.P.R.*, vol. xxi., October 1923, p. 139.

[2] See *Light*, June 21, 1924.

1884—yet the high position and respect the S.P.R. has won is chiefly due to Sidgwick, Myers, and Gurney, the three great pillars upon which the edifice of our Society was originally built. These eminent men were unlike in many ways : Sidgwick by his adhesion to the S.P.R. greatly impressed the academic world, for his influence, wisdom, and caution were widely recognised ; Myers by his enthusiasm, brilliant talents, and profound intuition, was the corner stone of the S.P.R. till his death in 1901 : Gurney with his industry and immense range of knowledge was essential to the early progress and stability of our Society.

Crookes was really the first scientific man to devote his experimental skill, from 1870 to 1874, to the critical investigation of the physical phenomena of spiritualism. It is pitiful to think of the scientific ostracism to which he was subjected and over which his genius eventually triumphed. I am not, however, surprised at the Royal Society refusing to publish his spiritistic investigations, for, a few years later, my modest paper read before the British Association in 1876 was refused publication by scientific societies, of which I was member, on the very natural ground that science dealt with the evidence furnished by our recognised senses, whereas my paper dealt either with phenomena which transcended the usual channels of sense or with phenomena that transcended the material world.

EARLY STEPS IN PSYCHICAL RESEARCH.

Many friends have asked me how I first became interested in psychical research. Perhaps I may be forgiven for relating an old story. Between the years 1862 and 1867 I was assistant to Professor Tyndall at the Royal Institution. The atmosphere surrounding my early years there was entirely opposed to any belief in psychical phenomena. Faraday, to whom electrical engineers owe the source of all their vast undertakings—yet who lived and died a poor man—Faraday I saw almost daily, before he left the Royal Institution and went to live at the Hampton

Court Cottage given to him by the Prince Consort. I can never forget the debt I owe that famous man for his generous kindness and guidance to a young ignoramus like myself. Faraday had published about 1855 his famous experiment on table-turning, showing how unconscious muscular effort accounted for what *he* saw. A little later he publicly declined to sit with the medium Home, saying he had lost too much time over such matters already. Tyndall also had denounced spiritualism as an imposture. Both Huxley and Herbert Spencer were frequent visitors to the Royal Institution laboratory, and both of these eminent men treated all psychical phenomena with contemptuous indifference. Among other frequent visitors was an Irishman, Mr. John Wilson, who invited me to spend my vacations at his place in County Westmeath. For a couple of years I did so, and found to my astonishment that Mr. Wilson was a firm believer in—and experienced investigator of—mesmerism, as it was then called. He showed me some most extraordinary experiments upon a sensitive subject from his estate. I was naturally incredulous and asked to be allowed to repeat the experiments myself, selecting another subject. We found a young uneducated Irish girl, who proved to be extremely sensitive. In the mesmeric trance—in spite of every precaution that I took to prevent deception—whatever sensations I felt, whether of touch, taste or smell, were transferred to the subject, and, moreover, ideas and words which I thought of were reproduced more or less accurately by the hypnotised subject. A brief account of some of these experiments may be found in the first volume of our *Proceedings*, p. 240.

When I returned to London I repeated these experiments with a couple of boys whom I found susceptible to hypnosis. These experiments revealed to me the extraordinary power of either verbal or silent suggestion upon the hypnotised subject. For instance, placing a pair of shoes upon the table, I told one of the lads that I was going to float round the room and pointed to the position I was supposed to have reached near the ceiling. Then, clapping my hands, I suggested that I was safely back in my shoes on the table. The boy stared at me with incredulity and related afterwards, both to me and to others, that he had really seen me floating round the room. A similar result was obtained by me with another subject when I was on a visit to America in 1884. Hence I was led to believe that spiritualistic phenomena, when not fraudulent, were really due to the *hallucination* of the observer ; that, in fact, the phenomena, such as Home floating out of the room or putting his hands into the fire, were really *subjective* and not objective. I had been in correspondence with Mr. Crookes on scientific matters so far back as the year 1864, when I published in the *Philosophical Magazine* my first scientific research. In 1870 Crookes began his experiments with the famous medium D. D. Home ; soon after this he wrote to me (in a letter which I have kept) as follows :

" May 14, 1871.

DEAR MR. BARRETT,

I must have some conversation with you respecting these obscure phenomena. If you can help me to form anything like a physical theory I should be delighted. At present all I am quite certain about is that they are *objectively* true. I have had all my wits about me when at a seance, and the only person who appeared to be in a state of semi-consciousness is the medium himself. The other evening I saw Home handling red-hot coals as if they had been oranges. Will you favour me with a visit one evening when you are disengaged.

Very truly yours,

WILLIAM CROOKES."

I had several interviews with Crookes, but unfortunately had no opportunity of any sitting with Home, and a year or two later I was appointed to the Chair of Physics at the Royal College of Science, Dublin. In 1874 I made my first acquaintance with the physical phenomena of spiritualism, and was able to put to the test my preconceived theory of hallucination, which was gradually dispelled, and I became convinced of the *objective* reality of the phenomena. It so happened that one of the London weekly reviews had sent me about this time a number of books on spiritualism to review, and in a lengthy review I suggested the hallucination hypothesis, but in a postscript added that this view was open to serious doubt.

The record of my experiments in Ireland on the physical phenomena of spiritualism was read before the S.P.R., and will be found in our *Proceedings*, vol. iv., p. 25, etc. I was singularly fortunate in these early experiments on physical phenomena, as the mediums were personal friends, and the experiments took place in *full light* either in my own house or in that of my friends. After this lapse of time I think I may mention without indiscretion that the name of the young medium I called Florrie was Miss Clark; her father, a leading London solicitor, had taken a furnished house near my residence in Kingstown. The house belonged to Mr. James Wilson (brother of my Westmeath friend), who asked me to call on Mr. Clark. Mr. Wilson was the father of the late Commander-in-Chief, Sir Henry Wilson, an old student of mine. My prolonged investigation of Florrie Clark, in *full daylight*, and other experiments with the family of the Lauders (one of the leading photographers in Dublin), so impressed me with the supreme importance of the whole subject that I determined to let no opportunity pass of pursuing these investigations. Shortly afterwards I prepared a paper on the various psychical phenomena I had witnessed; this was accepted by and read before the British Association in 1876.[1]

Verbatim reports of my paper were given both in the local and the spiritualist journals of Sept. 1876.[2] It will be seen from the reports of this paper that, while some notable scientific men such as Dr. W. B. Carpenter vigorously opposed my paper, others still more notable spoke in my support; such, for example, as Mr. (afterwards Sir William) Crookes and the late Lord Rayleigh (both of whom

[1] The greater part of this paper (which the British Association refused to publish) will be found in *Proceedings of the S.P.R.*, vol. i., p. 238 et seq.

[2] These are preserved in a scrap-book, which I still have.

subsequently became Presidents of the Royal Society), also the president of the Section, Mr. A. R. Wallace, and the distinguished anthropologist Col. Lane Fox, who afterwards became General Pitt-Rivers. I may add that a warm letter in support of my paper was received by me from the famous astronomer who subsequently became Sir William Huggins, also a President of the Royal Society.[1] The main object of my paper was a plea for a scientific committee to examine the validity of the evidence that I had adduced on behalf of what appeared to be thought-transference and other supernormal phenomena, especially those relating to spiritualism. Unfortunately, in the violent dispute which followed between Carpenter and Wallace, my resolution was lost sight of.

For weeks a great controversy ensued in the London *Times*, which, like all the other newspapers (with the exception of the *Spectator*), poured ridicule upon my daring to bring such a contemptible subject before the British Association. Among other of my vigorous opponents in *The Times* were Professors Lankester and Donkin (now Sir Ray and Sir Bryan); both of these distinguished men are still living and have not abated their hostility to the subject. Here it is interesting to note that in 1876 I ventured to state in *The Times* that before we could hope to arrive at any definite conclusion as to the origin of spiritualistic phenomena, we must first ascertain whether such a thing as the transfusion of thought between sitter and medium really existed and its extent; and, secondly, whether such a thing as clairvoyance or a transcendental perceptive power had any foundation in fact? Both these questions have now been answered in the affirmative, and this renders the above caution the more necessary.

'Book tests' show that Richet's theory of cryptesthesia, which seems to be another name for clairvoyance, needs serious consideration. The critical examination of Stainton Moses' script by our member Mr. Trethewy has shown that many apparently spirit communications are transcripts

---

[1] It is interesting to note that of the few scientific men who then had the courage to support my B.A. paper, no less than four received the Order of Merit.

of some matter which had been written or printed, it
may be long ago, and, as a rule, only to be found in
places inaccessible to the medium. *Nothing* seems able to
elude the prying eyes of the transcendental self, whether
it be incarnate or discarnate. In many sittings of to-day
the same thing holds good.[1] For example, that excellent
but illiterate medium, Sloan, of Glasgow, when in a trance
state will often give details concerning a sitter whom he
has never seen before and whose name even he does not
know, yet in subsequent investigation many of the facts
stated by the medium will be found printed, either in
Who's Who or other books to which the medium appears
to have had no possibility of access.

Hence, with these and other facts known to us, we must
realize that, however trustworthy may be the *evidence* we
obtain of supernormal phenomena, the *interpretation* of that
evidence may in time alter—as our experience grows wider,
and our knowledge of human psychology more extensive
and profound. Albeit I am personally convinced that the
evidence we have published decidedly demonstrates (1) the
existence of a spiritual world, (2) survival after death,
and (3) of occasional communications from those who have
passed over.

It will be obvious that in the present paper I cannot
give even an outline of the evidence that has led me
to the foregoing conclusions. The so-called physical
phenomena afford striking evidence of amazing supernormal power, but no proof of the survival of human
personality can be derived from them. In fact, many
people believe that they are simply due to the 'psychic
force' of the medium and sitters; however, this is an
opinion I do not share. Even the so-called 'ectoplasm,'
which is seen issuing in certain cases from the body of
the medium and sometimes taking human shape, may
be attributed to some mysterious, unknown, and unconscious power possessed by the medium. There can be
little doubt that the source of the ectoplasm is in some
way derived from the human organism; but I believe

[1] The most amazing illustration of telesthesia, or travelling clairvoyance,
I have ever known I hope to read before the S.P.R. shortly.

an unseen and intelligent supernormal agency *external* to
the medium causes this ectoplasm to take definite forms
and apparent vitality. I myself have not had the opportunity of ever witnessing these ectoplastic phenomena,
and therefore I defer to the opinion of such experienced
and critical observers as the late Dr. Geley, Prof. Richet,
and others.

PHYSICAL PHENOMENA.

As regards the ordinary physical phenomena I have
had a long series of experiments with various mediums,
going back to the time of Dr. Slade in 1876. Slade
always sat with me in broad daylight, and though I
have little doubt that he not unfrequently resorted to
trickery, yet there was also no doubt he had genuine
and remarkable mediumistic powers ; his so-called exposure
by Prof. Ray Lankester was quite inconclusive. Those
who are interested in the matter will find in Stainton
Moses's *Psychography*, pp. 104-110, a record of some of
my experiments with Slade, in part quoted from the
London *Times* of September 1876, and also a careful
report written by my friend Mr. Conrad Cook, who
accompanied me to a sitting with Slade in August 1876.

The only case of ' materialization ' witnessed by me,
which seemed to be inexplicable by fraud, occurred with
the medium, Husk, many years ago. It may be worth
while describing this experiment as it has never been
published.

Mr. Wm. de Morgan had kindly lent Myers and myself
his studio in Cheyne Row, an almost bare room, furnished
with a small deal table about 3 feet by 5 feet, and a
few chairs. After dinner Myers brought Husk to Cheyne
Row in a hansom cab, and we immediately sat round
the table. There were six present including the medium.
William de Morgan and his sister (being sceptics), were
placed in control of the medium, whose feet were tied
to the legs of the table, and his hands were grasped by
the sitter on each side. Mrs. de Morgan (their mother),
sat facing Myers, and I sat at the other end of the

table and had control of the light. After the wrists of
all present had been loosely joined together by silk
thread, I blew out the candle and phenomena very soon
occurred. The medium went into a trance, lights, very
like fireflies, were seen darting about over our heads,
movement of some objects in the room was heard, and
a deep guttural voice spoke to us calling himself ' John
King.' In reply to our request he said he would try
and show himself. A violent convulsion of the medium
occurred, and suddenly right in front of me appeared a
clothed human figure from the waist upwards : the lower
part of the body might have been concealed by the
table. The face was illuminated by a bluish light which
seemed to issue from an object held in the hand of the
materialized figure. The face was undoubtedly a living
one, for I saw its eyes open and close and its lips move ;
I asked who it was and the guttural voice said " John
King." It was a dark bearded and rather unpleasant
face, quite unlike that of the medium. I exclaimed,
" Do you all see the figure ? I am going to light the
candle," and immediately risked doing so. The figure vanished
the moment the match was struck, and the medium
was found in deep trance, lying back in his chair and
groaning : when the medium had recovered he was sent
home in a cab. On comparing notes, each sitter described
the face according to the different aspects it presented
from his or her position at the table. We found upon
experimenting that it was impossible to reproduce the
figure by leaning over the table, nor could the medium
have put on a mask, as his hands were held the whole
time and the tying of his legs and wrists were found
intact. De Morgan asked Myers and myself to come
the next morning and see if we could in any way imitate
what we had seen. Though de Morgan remained somewhat
sceptical, Myers and I both agreed that it was extremely
difficult to explain the phenomena by trickery on the
part of the medium, who, moreover, was found deeply
entranced a few seconds later.

   With regard to the so-called ' spirit photographs,'
I have been extremely sceptical of their genuineness

until quite lately. Recently, however, experiments conducted by my friend Mr. de Brath, in one of which he kindly allowed me to take part, appear to afford *indubitable* evidence of supernormal psychic photography. This conclusion confirms the opinion held by some expert and critical experimenters, who have discussed their results with me. Of course faked ' spirit photographs ' abound and are easy to produce ; whilst heartless rascals exist who prey upon the grief of a credulous sitter. Healthy scepticism has therefore been inevitable and wise. But we shall never arrive at any knowledge of the conditions requisite for these and other marvellous psychic phenomena, until hostile incredulity becomes no longer possible. Then, as Sir John Herschel says, " occurrences which, according to received theories *ought not* to happen, are the *facts* which serve as clues to new discoveries." [1]

These disputable subjects illustrate the importance of our society recognizing the fact that a difference of opinion— a *right* and a *left* wing—will necessarily have to exist among its different members. I mean that there are some who have been convinced at first hand, from their own experience, that the existence of certain psychical phenomena—especially those associated with spiritualism—admit of no doubt whatever, and are impatient with those who have not had this experience and are therefore more inclined to be cautious and even sceptical. The former class of our members wish to push forward and perhaps attach less importance to conclusive experimental evidence than they did at first : the latter class wish to go much more slowly and proceed step by step. This difference of opinion, though healthy, naturally leads to a divergence of interest in our subject, and from time to time threatens to break up the solidarity of our society.

Nor must we forget that psychical research, as stated in the original articles of our society, embraces far more than spiritistic phenomena, and I hope that our research officers will ever bear in mind the varied objects of our

[1] *Discourse on Natural Philosophy*, section 5.

society, which will be found printed in the first volume of our *Proceedings*.

Personally I am very anxious that earnest attention should be given to the so-called ' Reichenbach Phenomena,' wherein certain sensitives after long immersion in complete darkness perceive a luminosity emanating from the poles of a magnet and also from the human fingers. I have published in the *Philosophical Magazine*, and also in the early volumes of our *Proceedings*, the experiments which led me to the conviction that such phenomena do really occur under suitable conditions.

Another point, which I hope will sooner or later be the subject of further experiment, is the question of the old mesmeric hypothesis of ' effluence,' for which both Gurney and myself obtained what appeared to be satisfactory evidence forty years ago, and which Prof. Alrutz has in recent years confirmed.

The immediate work before us is to convince scientific authorities that various types of supernormal phenomena do *really* exist, and are capable of experimental proof. I do not think that the indifference of official science to our investigation, which has now replaced their former hostility, will be affected by an appeal to the *emotions*, such as the evidence obtained of survival after death. Science will approach the supernormal from an entirely different angle ; it may possibly be pulled over the line of its present indifference by a growing recognition that telepathy does really exist. Unfortunately, the difficulty of finding suitable subjects both for telepathy and telesthesia is a great drawback. For this reason I am led to the conviction that the first movement of thought of official science in our direction will occur from the impossibility of finding any *normal* explanation of the phenomena of *dowsing*. And this subject is of all others the simplest and easiest to investigate. It has not only a wide practical importance, but it raises no religious opposition, even from the most timid of narrow-minded people. Moreover, the number of efficient dowsers can easily be ascertained and experimented with. Having devoted more than twenty years to the critical investigation of this subject, I believe that it affords the easiest and most conclusive evidence that a supernormal perceptive power—akin to clairvoyance—exists in certain persons, of either sex, of all ages and all degrees of education.

This faculty is to be found not only in various races of men, but appears to exist, as a new and necessary sense, in many of the lower types of life. I am convinced that the mysterious migration of birds, even of very young ones, over vast tracts of land and sea, and also the *homing* instincts of many birds and animals, will be found to be akin to the dowsing faculty in man.[1]

DIFFERENCE BETWEEN PHYSICAL AND PSYCHICAL RESEARCH.

There is, of course, a fundamental difference between physical research and psychical research. The former deals with matter and energy, and the condition of the mind of the observer, whether he be sceptical or not, is of no consequence. The latter deals with the phenomena of the subconscious, and the mental attitude both of the experimenter and his subject, is of prime importance. An interesting illustration of the difference between the mental states in the two cases occurred to me some time ago. I happened to be staying in Edinburgh with that famous physicist, Professor Tait, when the news of the discovery of the telephone came to us by cable. I asked Tait what he thought of it. He replied, "It is all humbug, for such a discovery is physically impossible." When I asked him how it was that well-known men had asserted that they had heard speech transmitted a couple of miles through a wire, Tait replied it was "probably a case of the conduction of sound by long straight wires." A little later, when the telephone was shown at the British Association by Sir W. Thomson (afterwards Lord Kelvin) and experiments with it were successfully made, Tait's obstinate incredulity did not interfere with the success of the experiment. A similar instance occurred in Paris when the

[1] See Chapter Two of my little book *Creative Thought*, published by Watkins, Cecil Court, London, W.C.

Abbé Moigno, a well-known scientific writer, first showed Edison's phonograph to the Paris Academy of Sciences; the Abbé himself related to me what occurred. All the *savants* present declared, as Professor Tait did, that the reproduction of the human voice by an iron disc was physically impossible owing to the subtle wave forms produced by speech, though they admitted music might be so transmitted. The Abbé was even accused of having a ventriloquist concealed beneath the table. He left the chamber in disgust and told them to try the instrument themselves—which they did quite successfully in spite of their utter incredulity.

How different is the effect that is produced by mental environment in psychical phenomena is well known. Those experienced observers, Stainton Moses and C. C. Massey, have said, "the most unfavourable disposition to take to a medium is suspicion, and the most favourable is confidence." Sceptics may think that this is to deliver oneself over as a prey to the deceiver, and some men do certainly get taken in, but experience after a time leads them to discover their mistake. In the psychical world "faith," as Mr. Massey says, "is a condition of obtaining evidence, the key to the gate of the invisible world." By faith Massey means that a *sympathetic* state of mind establishes a rapport between the observer and the medium. The fact that we need no sympathy with our instruments, when testing a physical or chemical discovery, naturally leads the physicist or chemist to a state of scornful amusement, when told that his own attitude of mind is of importance in psychical research. But it appears to be a fact that even if at the back of our minds we entertain feelings of prejudice and hostility, we can hope for little success in psychic enquiry, however much we may disclaim the feeling of hostility. This, of course, does not mean an attitude of credulity or any relaxation of careful and critical observation.

All psychical researchers need to bear in mind that every sensitive or medium is a *suggestible subject*; if you go expecting fraud you may possibly create the very fraud you suspect. If you make preparations beforehand to lay a trap for the medium, it is probable that both medium and experimenter will fall into the trap.

There is another aspect of our enquiry, known to most of us—that is, that psychical phenomena largely depend upon involuntary and not voluntary effort, upon the subconscious and not the conscious self. Even in the simple phenomena of telepathy it is the subliminal self that is operative. Further, I believe that the common practice of experimenters *energetically willing* the idea to be thought of, is of no value, and may indeed be detrimental to success. In the early experiments which Myers, Gurney, and myself conducted with the Creery children at Buxton we found that the best results occurred when no strenuous efforts were made. In fact, when we made the experiments as amusing as possible, we had the greatest success, though every precaution was taken to prevent collusion or signalling.

Another fact which seems to me brought out very clearly in our experiments is that psychical phenomena, whether of telepathy, clairvoyance, or the higher phenomena of spiritualism, are manifestations of, or through, the *transcendental self* of the subject, and are therefore independent of the fundamental units of the physical world—matter, time, and space. It is true that, in the case of telepathy, the mental response of the percipient to the idea in the agent's mind, naturally suggests the physical analogue of the resonance of a silent tuning-fork to a sounding one which is in perfect unison with it. Indeed, I was inclined at first to think that telepathy was somewhat similar to this—that it was a *nervous induction* across space, analogous to the well-known facts of electric and magnetic induction. But whilst telepathy has been made more conceivable, and more credible to the public generally, by the discovery and use of wireless telephony, we must remember that the two phenomena are wholly different. One belongs to the *physical* order, the other to the *psychical* order. The laws regulating the transmission of energy across space apply to the one, but not to the other. Immense effort is necessary to transmit a wireless message across the Atlantic, but apparently no effort at all is required to transmit a telepathic impact, of which we have instances, from New Zealand to London. On the contrary, a *passive* condition of both transmitter and receiver in telepathy seems essential, so far at least as their consciousness is concerned.

The word 'thought-transference' is apt to be misleading, as it seems to suggest a transmission of ideas between two persons across material space ; but, as I said, space does not seem to enter into the question at all. Here it may be interesting to note that in the first publication of the discovery of this super-sensuous faculty, I called it not 'thought-transference,' but the *transfusion of thought.*[1] We are now coming back to this idea, for telepathy is probably the intermingling of our transcendental selves or souls. The common and grossly materialistic conception of the soul is that it is limited to the confines and contour of the body. This is surely an erroneous conception if, as we believe, the soul is an *immaterial* entity, not simply a function of the brain. For all we know to the contrary, the human soul may spread through a vast orbit around the body, and may intermingle with other incarnate or discarnate souls. Tennyson speaks of a dream condition, "when the mortal limit of the self was loosed, and past into the Nameless, as the cloud melts into Heaven." Moreover the intimacy and immediacy of the union between the soul and God is the fundamental idea, not only of the New Testament, but of all great Christian thinkers.

CONCLUSION.

As evidence of the great value which some eminent men attached to our investigations at their very outset, I will only quote from a couple of letters which I received more than forty years ago. That distinguished scientific man of the last generation, Dr. Angus Smith, F.R.S., writing to me in 1876, on the theoretic importance of thought-transference, remarked that "the indications now obtained point

---

[1] See *Proceedings, S.P.R.,* vol. i., p. 48, where will be found an extract from a letter of mine to *The Times* dated Sept. 1876.

to some mighty truth more decidedly than even the aberrations of Uranus to the newest of the great planets. If we could prove the action of mind at a distance by constant experiments it would be a discovery that would make all other discoveries seem trifles." This was also the view of that eminent biologist, Mr. G. J. Romanes, F.R.S., who, when writing to me on the same subject in 1881, remarked "if the alleged phenomena are true I hold it to be unquestionable that they would be of more importance than any other in the science and philosophy of our time."

Quite recently our former President, Professor W. M'Dougall, F.R.S., in his presidential address to the American S.P.R. speaks of psychical research as the most hopeful barrier against the oncoming tide of materialism, and he remarks that "a civilization which resigns itself wholly to materialism lives upon and consumes its moral capital and is incapable of renewing it. . . . Unless psychical research can discover facts incompatible with materialism, materialism will continue to spread ; no other power can stop it, both revealed religion and metaphysical philosophy are equally helpless before the advancing tide." As regards religion being helpless, I cannot, however, go as far as M'Dougall.

Richet's point of view, which is purely materialistic, appears at first to contradict M'Dougall's remarks. We know that Richet, with splendid courage and loyalty to truth, has avowed his belief in the most incredible psychical phenomena, some of which even we may perhaps hesitate to accept. But Richet's philosophy compels him to reject the spiritualistic hypothesis and to explain everything by a modified psychic force theory ; a theory which was once accepted by Crookes but subsequently rejected by him. Richet attributes all the subjective phenomena of psychical research to 'cryptesthesia,' and some of the objective to 'pragmatic cryptesthesia.' [1] But these polysyllables do not

[1] Richet uses this term instead of psychometry (soul measurement), which he rightly says is so detestable a word that he proposes to call it "pragmatic cryptesthesia, *i.e.* cryptesthesia by means of material objects."

help us any more than the names given by some learned psychologists who tell us that all psychical phenomena are simply illustrations of the "exteriorised effects of unconscious complexes!" One is reminded by this formidable nomenclature of the numerous and recondite hypotheses by which Ptolemaic astronomers tried to make their observations square with the geocentric theory of the universe. To the plain man it seems simpler, less 'improbable and more in accordance with facts, for biologists to recognise —what astronomers long since have done—that the universe after all is *not* explicable from the restricted view-point either of the earth or of the brain. Nevertheless, Richet's views will doubtless form the half-way house of many *savants* who hold mechanistic theories of the universe. However, I venture to predict that neither they nor Richet will remain many years in that convenient but anomalous resting-place.

Sooner or later psychical research will demonstrate to the educated world, not only the existence of a *soul in man*, but also the existence of a *soul in Nature*. Our biologists have hitherto been so largely wedded to materialistic views that they have overlooked the vast importance of the psychic factor in evolution. The recognition of such a purposive and a pervasive factor, running throughout the whole realm of nature, will be found necessary to invoke in order to explain many biological phenomena that now receive very inadequate solution from current theories. Long ago Lord Kelvin said, " Overpoweringly strong proofs exist of intelligence and benevolent design in Nature."

At the present day, when the very foundations of religion appear to be shaken, and men are deserting the faith of their fathers, and the whole civilised world is becoming more and more materialistic in its views, it is evident that psychical research will ere long be regarded, by all thoughtful men, as the most valuable handmaid to religion. Scarcely a week passes without my receiving letters or visits from perplexed men, both among the clergy and laity, who have found their religious creeds crumbling beneath their feet, and want to know what help they might obtain from psychical research. Mr. Gladstone's opinion on, this subject is well known and often quoted; and Frederic Myers, as we know, has eloquently expressed his views. In his *Human Personality* again and again he returns to this aspect of the subject, and in his last chapter remarks, "We do not seek to shape the clauses of the great Act of Faith, but merely to prove its *preamble*. . . . To be able to say to the theologian or philosopher : 'Thus and thus we demonstrate that a spiritual world exists—a world of independent and abiding realities, not a mere epi-phenomenon or transitory effect of the material world—but a world of *things*, concrete and living; not a mere system of abstract ideas' . . . "; and he adds, "This would indeed, in my view, be the weightiest service that *any* research could render to the deep disquiet of our time—to the world-old, and world-wide, desire "[1] of mankind.

[1] *Human Personality*, vol. ii., p. 297.

* 9 7 9 8 8 8 6 7 7 0 3 0 8 *